THE DRAMA AND
THE STAGE

THE DRAMA AND THE STAGE

BY

LUDWIG LEWISOHN

Essay Index Reprint Series

BOOKS FOR LIBRARIES PRESS
FREEPORT, NEW YORK

First Published 1922
Reprinted 1969

STANDARD BOOK NUMBER:
8369-1089-3

LIBRARY OF CONGRESS CATALOG CARD NUMBER:
71-84319

PRINTED IN THE UNITED STATES OF AMERICA

Prefatory Note

THE brief essays and studies that compose this volume are desultory only in appearance. They were written on, but not for a particular day, and seek to illustrate, whatever the date or the material, a theory of both the drama and the theatre that is coherent and that is profoundly implicated with permanent qualities of life and art. They all had their first appearance in the *Nation*, to the editor of which, Mr. Oswald Garrison Villard, I am indebted, among many other things, for his permission to reprint them here.

L. L.

CONTENTS

I. THE NEW DRAMATURGY

II. THE AMERICAN STAGE

III. CONTEMPORARIES

IV. ART, LIFE AND THE THEATRE

I
Toward a New Dramaturgy

The Drama and the Stage

THE critical observer of our living theatre, to be useful at all, must cultivate good humor, patience and tolerance. To great humility of expectation and a gratitude for small mercies he must add a steadfast determination not to be taken in. For the theatre is a place of many illusions, the home of over-eager minds and of harsh ambitions, the scene of an alternation of blazing splendor and of bleak despair. No one can understand the theatre who sees it too intently from within; no one can serve it who does not, as it is to-day, hold it a little cheap. Because the theatre of to-day is being killed—by the theatre. This mechanism which, stripped to its essentials, is but a wooden platform sheltered from the winds, this simple thing placed now on a hill-side, now in an inn-yard, now in a room, has become an end in itself. Revolving stages, subtle lights, elaborate scenes are in their right order beautiful and useful things. They become a menace when they cause it to be forgotten that the platform is the platform of the eternal poet struggling with the mysteries of the earth. This is not fine language; it is the plain and sober truth. But who will admit it? David Belasco? Or the hundred mechanics of the

3

theatre who will swear to you that John Galsworthy may be a dramatist for the study but that he doesn't understand the theatre?

As if, indeed, there were anything so intricate to understand! But this trumped-up technical intricacy of play-writing is the bread and butter as well as the chief pride of its adepts—adepts of a delusion which they uphold to save their trade and their self-importance. Learned men have come to their aid, interpreting the transformations of that ancient platform as the history of the drama; poets have abetted them by innocent fear and wonder. Yet that delusion crumbles at the most obvious test. On the stage, as it is to-day, we have seen the *Medea* of Euripides and the Book of Job; we have seen *Everyman;* we have seen Shakespeare; we have seen Ibsen and Hauptmann, Galsworthy and Shaw, and the fantasies of Maeterlinck and Dunsany. Which of these understood that mysterious mechanism? Which of them had that esoteric sense for what is "of the theatre"?

Let us have done, first of all then, with this verbiage.

A play is a dialogue which, when spoken by actors from a platform, holds the minds of men through its culmination toward some physical or spiritual end.

The power and depth of that sense of culmination is the measure of the play's dramatic life.

Any dialogue that has dramatic life can be acted on any stage.

A born dramatist can write drama without ever having seen a theatre. If an audience refuses to hear him, it is because the soul of his work is alien from that audience's collective soul.

The popular playwright is not he who understands either the theatre or the drama best, but he who flatters men most and disturbs them least.

It is in the intellectual character of the audience, not in the mechanism of the theatre or the technique of writing plays, that the causes for the condition of our stage are to be sought. From a platform you cannot speak to one man; you speak to many. And the group is always less intelligent, less flexible, less merciful than the individual. The hope of the theatre is in the fact that there are groups and groups. A group has been found to keep *Jane Clegg* in a New York play-house for many consecutive weeks. But since the commercial managers seek not the best group but the largest, the staple of our stage is sodden melodrama and brainless farce. The serviceable critic will try to rally the smaller groups and sustain their contact with the more civilized enterprises of the theatre.

The Theatre: Mythical and Real [1]

In the cities of the East and of the West Mr. Gordon Craig would have theatres arise that are also temples. They are to be majestic but not cold; in them are to blend the precious glow and glint of gold and ivory and jade. Within and without they are to be durable and changeless in their massive beauty. Upon their stages the scenery is to consist of wrought and carven symbols. There is to be nothing perishable, nor anything that too closely recalls the perishable. By mellow daylight actors from whom "all weaknesses of the flesh have been eradicated," wearing masks, or—since even these actors are but a concession—Uebermarionettes are to perform a silent and universal drama. And Mr. Craig has, no doubt, a vision of faithful multitudes streaming upon appointed holy days to these temples, hushed with awe and wonder before the splendor of their mysteries.

Well, Mr. Craig is mistaken. No multitudes would come to his temples, but only a few forlorn and feebly irritable esthetes and reactionaries. It is not the durableness and lofty beauty of his theatres that will keep the multitude away. For the barbarous multitude will

[1] *The Theatre—Advancing.* By Edward Gordon Craig.

6

go as gladly to a temple as to a barn to see a play.
But it demands a play. And at this point Mr. Craig's
beautiful and imaginative vision suddenly exhibits a
staring gap. What is the play to be about? Granted
that it is to be a super-pantomime acted by austere
men or marionettes, it must express something; it must
tell something. The content of that play, so far as Mr.
Craig permits us dimly to gather and infer, is to symbolize by universal gestures the inner mystery of what
is man and the world and God. But in order to symbolize that mystery in art so clearly and universally
that men shall flock to his vast rituals, the dramatist
must first have solved it. And his solution must com-
mend itself to all. He must, in other words, first reës-
tablish an historic condition analogous to that of the
thirteenth century in which the eternal mysteries are
held to have been finally explained and in which symbolical embodiments of this explanation are as welcome
in the market-place as in the sanctuary.

Of this necessity Mr. Craig is quite aware. He is
thoroughly consistent. He holds that "modern life is
damnable," that all our troubles have been brewed by
the Materialist Fool, that what we lack is "belief and
the power to worship." He thinks that a mob is an ugly
thing and a king a beautiful one; he is wholly innocent
of the desperate materialism of his own thought. "Hail
once more," he exclaims, "to that divine arrogance
which knew that the obedience of the many to the judg-

ments of the one meant happiness to the mass of men."
He thinks that the ancient Hindus' "love of loveliness
and sanity sprang from their love of obedience to their
arrogant rulers," and that if we can but revive their
awe and wonder and humility on earth then "States
and religions will arise all fresh once more and Mankind will again be happy." It is the old and amiable
delusion of the romantic dreamer who dreams an
ordered and beautiful and hierarchical world with himself, of course, stationed near the top of the hierarchy,
building the majestic temples of his vision, and never
picturing himself as one of the obedient multitude
whom it pleases him to imagine hanging upon his lips
and enthralled by the authority of his soul. If he once
did that his gorgeous vision, pinnacles and all, would
fade like a puff of smoke. For he would at once dis-
cover in his own heart the eternal heretic and rebel
who has but to arise and to reflect to know that it is
the essence of his manhood to be free. Whatever, then,
may be Mr. Craig's gifts as a scenic artist and stage
craftsman—and they are, doubtless, of the highest—it
is clear that his theories of the theatre have been treated
far more gravely than they deserve.

What Mr. Craig, in fact, succeeds in doing is to
leave us with a feeling of unwonted tenderness and
charity toward that actual theatre at which, for the
best reasons possible, we may just have been jeering.
For that theatre, more in some countries than in oth-

ers, but a little everywhere, tries to fulfil its true function and to serve mankind in its appointed way. It is
the way of all art which, sometimes aiming after the
illusion of the real, sometimes by a synthesis of the
elements of experience, clarifies and interprets our
world for us, shows forth its hidden meaningfulness
and beauty, and thus, by persuading the individual to
rise, through the contemplation of the concrete, to a
larger vision, takes from him the burden of the pain
and confusion of life. It does for him precisely what
the creative act does for the poet. The latter transfers
his experience to the objective world and gives it form
and meaning. He then sees it apart from himself under
some eternal aspect and is free of its tyrannies and
fears. We others, contemplating the poet's works in
the study or on the stage, are liberated by them and
raised above ourselves in just the measure in which they
hold and interpret human experiences that we too have
known and have endured. Hence to increase the dignity and worth and appeal of any art, including the art
of the theatre, it is necessary (whether the technical
method be naturalistic or idealistic) to bring it ever
closer and closer to the concrete realities of man's struggle with himself and with his world. Mr. Craig wants
to create first a new mythology and then a new ritual
in his durable theatres. What the sane friends of the
theatre desire is to strip it of those remnants of the old
mythologies and rituals that still so often make it a

tawdry and a shameful thing. Mr. Craig wants a drama of faith. Let him go to see the melodramas. There he will find fierce tribal faiths and age-long delusions of hatred and terror still at their ancient business of intolerance and persecution and self-righteousness and force. There he will learn that, if he were to build his theatre-temples in his new order, and free spirits were to build still other theatres, the kings and sacerdotal managers of his dim shrines would soon be at their old tricks of burning both the non-conformist and his house.

The problem of improving or, if you will, reforming the living theatre is, in truth, neither so intricate nor so esoteric as Mr. Craig and a few other theorists would have us believe. The theatre on the Continent of Europe has been, for rather more than thirty years, in a very tolerable condition. In no city of any considerable size in France or Germany or Austria or Switzerland or Holland or Scandinavia has a season gone by without many adequate representations of the works of the modern masters or a few dignified and intelligent revivals of the classics of all countries. For a variety of reasons, some obscure enough, some clear to any observer, the theatre of the English-speaking countries lags behind. The immediate practical problem is obvious: to work towards a condition of our theatre and its audiences in which Shakespeare and Sheridan, Galsworthy and Shaw will be as gladly and as widely heard as Molière and Goethe, Ibsen and Hauptmann, Hervieu and Schnitzler are heard in their respective countries. That problem, assuredly, will not be solved, it will not even be touched, by an amiable and gifted mystic who flies in the face of historic processes.

The Critic and the Theatre

If there is one person, we are often tempted to assert, who should not be permitted to criticize the drama, it is the dramatic critic. It is not because he commonly fails of being sensitive, honest, and even learned. It is because his profession puts him in a false position. Consider for a moment the man's task. He must be, on command, in a receptive mood toward the most complex of all the arts. But his receptivity must be controlled from the start by a conscientious inner censorship of his impressions. He sees to report and enjoys to dissect. The wise passiveness which is the condition of fine artistic judgment is not for him. He cannot, like the critic of literature, attack his document again, reflect and reconsider, and correct his morning mood by his midnight one. He must grasp his bright, brief, transitory pageant at once, and he must grasp it, ideally, with the imaginative innocence of a child, the austere detachment of a philosopher, the rich sympathies of a man. For the poorest play, feeble and foolish though it be, is in its very nature plastic vision, philosophy and life. It is vision, obviously, through its mobile and colorful embodiment on the stage; it is philosophy, since every dramatic action culminates in an ending which betrays the playwright's attitude to the totality of things; it is life by being an example of an art of imitation. No wonder, then, that the dramatic critic, jaded by his round of enforced appreciation on the one hand, or unable, on the other, to keep so many psychical balls in the air, either hides the nobler part of him and deals in trenchant, critical detail, the flash of wit, the exploitation of his personality, or that, like an unskilful juggler, he drops the balls, denies their existence, and flees for permanent refuge to a theory that artificially simplifies the art he contemplates and reduces his function to something more agreeable with mortal powers. Thus we have brilliant comment on this or that aspect of the theatre, but comment that is, in any larger sense, quite sterile. Or else we have learned and charming and urbane exercitations upon all externals of theatrical and dramatic history and practice, which leave the core of the matter quite untouched. We have *Hamlet* with the critic substituting himself for the protagonist; we have *Hamlet* with Hamlet left out.

There is Mr. George Jean Nathan.[1] That he sometimes makes the judicious wince and often makes the fastidious shudder is a small matter. For he has some of the qualifications of a dramatic critic in a higher degree than any other American contemporary. He

[1] *Comedians All.* By George Jean Nathan.

has an unrivaled knowledge of the modern stage, a
thorough impatience with sham and cant, and flashes
—as in his brief note on the artificial play—of the most
searching insight.   But because sentimentality and
sweetishness and foolish uplift have so often among us
masqueraded as serious art, he has huddled everything
that seeks to touch the soul, the genuine as well as the
false, into one basket and flung that basket out of his
back window.   What he wants is intelligent entertainment, plays that will please a comfortable and discriminating man of the world.   He will not get what he
wants, and much of his fine energy will have been spent
quite in vain.   No man can write a serious play, and
show men and women acting and suffering, except upon
spiritual and moral terms, except with attitudes, opinions, and principles that reveal his inmost soul even
more than theirs and bind the playwright and his play
to stern and fundamental things.   The drama is, quite
literally, what Aristotle called all poetry—more philosophical than history.   Do *Œdipus Rex* and *Hamlet*
afford intelligent entertainment, or—to come to Mr.
Nathan's special field—*An Enemy of the People* or
The Weavers or *The Lower Depths?*   The intelli-
gently entertaining play, which commonly assumes the
form of polite comedy, is the product of small, compact, untroubled communities.   Such the vast seethings
of the world's life tolerate less and less.   Mr. Nathan,
in a word, has no patience with tinsel and paper flow-

ers. He finds them out with an unerring gaze and with a cold exuberant enjoyment reduces them to pulp. But the theatre cannot be helped by the mere exposure of isolated instances of hollowness and fraud, even though that exposure be full of energy and wit and good sense. As the playwright inevitably reveals his special perception of ultimate values in his plays, so the dramatic critic, speaking of those plays, betrays the road of the mind upon which he travels. And Mr. Nathan's pilgrimage, unless we mistake him grossly, is—towards orchids. He wants to sit quietly in his aloof and faunlike elegance and glance at the exquisite form and glow of the petals and forget annoying things, and, through a succession of such experiences, build a house of art in which he can be secure from the tyranny of the Puritan and the contamination of the mob. But never was the theatre less likely than to-day to become a gentleman's Paradise. We must either acquiesce in its present sentimentality and gaudiness—and that a man of Mr. Nathan's sophistication cannot do—or else we must cast in our lot with the world process and seek to bring the gravest and most stirring of the arts nearer, in its true character, to an ever-increasing number of men—and that Mr. Nathan will not do. Thus it comes about that, with all its vehemence and strength and veracity in detail, Mr. Nathan's critical structure is built of fragile materials in a precarious and a lonely place.

Professor Brander Matthews,[1] through his teaching
and writing, through his unfailing vivacity and accomplished scholarship, has probably done more to touch
the minds of intelligent people with a vivid interest in
the theatre than any other living American. If he has
not helped the American theatre itself as powerfully
as, given his station and influence, he might have done,
it is because he has too often acquiesced in its condition upon a somewhat rigid application of certain
historical analogies. These analogies he reiterates in
The Principles of Playmaking. Since Shakespeare and
Molière were, first of all, successful playwrights, who
made an immediate appeal to the audiences of their
day, Professor Matthews makes such an appeal the
criterion of the dramatist of all ages. But Shakespeare
and Molière wrote for very small and homogeneous
audiences. To which of the innumerable audiences of
a contemporary metropolis, it must be asked, shall the
young dramatist address himself? Whose applause
shall decide whether he makes an analogous appeal in
his own time and place—that of the audiences of some
bed-room farce, or of the Theatre Guild? And how
long a run shall, for a given play, constitute its test of
that broad popularity which we rightly grant Shakespeare and Molière on the score of a few performances? Nor is it always true to-day that the "audience
is a crowd composed of all sorts and conditions of

[1] *Principles of Playmaking*. By Brander Matthews.

men." A New York audience, for instance, is composed of people who can achieve a certain standard of dress, who can risk—with galleries abolished and balconies restricted—two dollars on an evening's entertainment or boredom, who belong neither to the great religious communions that disapprove of the theatre, nor to that very cultivated minority which, in its present state, disdains it. Hence our playwright, far from being obliged to "deal with subjects appealing to collective human nature," must, for immediate success, cater to the tastes and prejudices of a narrow, inflexible, commonly over-fed bourgeoisie, desperately frightened by ideas and unfamiliar modes of feeling. Thus the phrase of Molière, "to please the public," has little left in common with its original meaning, and every first-rate modern dramatist has had to help destroy the contemporary theatre as he found it in order to be heard at all. So soon as we grasp the true nature of these conditions, the entire theory which differentiates the secondary literary qualities of a play from its primary theatrical ones collapses. To the right audience, once it be found and gathered, a notable drama's excellence in invention, structure and style will constitute its theatrical effectiveness; its "veracity of character" will afford all needed "histrionic opportunities" —who would desire opportunities that do not grow out of such veracity?—and its truth to the human environment with which it deals will be picturesque enough.

No, it is not acquiescence from which the most fruitful criticism can arise. Our theatre is not, so far as it is most prosperous, the theatre of the great dramatists fallen upon evil days. It is the theatre of a class and an economic condition from which we must free it for the service of nobler and more human things.

A Note on Tragedy

It has been said many times, and always with an air of authority, that there is no tragedy in the modern drama. And since tragedy, in the minds of most educated people, is hazily but quite firmly connected with the mishaps of noble and mythical personages, the statement has been widely accepted as true. Thus very tawdry Shakespearean revivals are received with a traditional reverence for the sternest and noblest of all the art-forms that is consciously withheld from *Ghosts* or *Justice* or *The Weavers*. Placid people in college towns consider these plays painful. They hasten to pay their respects to awkward chantings of Gilbert Murray's Swinburnian verses and approve the pleasant mildness of the pity and terror native to the Attic stage. The very innocuousness of these entertainments as well as the pain that Ibsen and Hauptmann inflict should give them pause. Pity and terror are strong words and stand for strong things. But our public replies in the comfortable words of its most respectable critics that tragedy has ceased to be written.

These critics reveal a noteworthy state of mind. They are aware that tragedy cuts to the quick of life and springs from the innermost depth of human thinking because it must always seek to deal in some

intelligible way with the problem of evil. But since it
is most comfortable to believe that problem to have
been solved, they avert their faces from a reopening
of the eternal question and declare that the answer of
the Greeks and the Elizabethans is final. They are
also aware, though more dimly, that all tragedy involves moral judgments. And since they are unaccus-
tomed to make such judgments, except by the light of
standards quite rigid and quite antecedent to experience, they are bewildered by a type of tragic drama
that transfers its crises from the deeds of men to the
very criteria of moral judgment, from guilt under a law
to the arraignment of the law itself.

Macbeth represents in art and life their favorite
tragic situation. They can understand a gross and
open crime meeting a violent punishment. When as
in *King Lear,* the case is not so plain, they dwell long
and emphatically on the old man's weaknesses in order
to find satisfaction in his doom. In the presence of
every tragic protagonist of the modern drama they are
tempted to play the part of Job's comforters. They
are eager to impute to him an absoluteness of guilt
which shall, by implication, justify their own moral
world and the doctrine of moral violence by which they
live. The identical instinct which in war causes men
to blacken the enemy's character in order to justify
their tribal rage and hate, persuades the conventional
critic to deny the character of tragedy to every action

in which disaster does not follow upon crime. Yet, rightly looked upon, man in every tragic situation is a Job, incapable and unconscious of any degree of voluntary guilt that can justify a suffering as sharp and constant as his own.

Thus modern tragedy does not deal with wrong and just vengeance, which are both, if conceived absolutely, pure fictions of our deep-rooted desire for superiority and violence. It is inspired by compassion. But compassion without complacency is still, alas, a very rare emotion. And it seeks to derive the tragic element in human life from the mistakes and self-imposed compulsions, not from the sins, of men. The central idea of *Ghosts*, for instance, is not concerned with the sin of the father that is visited upon the son. It is concerned, as Ibsen sought to make abundantly clear, with Mrs. Alving's fatal conformity to a social tradition that did not represent the pureness of her will. Her tragic mistake arises from her failure to break the law. The ultimate and absolute guilt is in the blind, collective lust of mankind for the formulation and indiscriminate enforcement of external laws.

To such a conception of the moral world, tragedy has but recently attained. That both the critical and the public intelligence should lag far behind is inevitable. Every morning's paper proclaims a world whose moral pattern is formed of terrible blacks and glaring whites. How should people gladly endure the endless and pain-touched gray of modern tragedy? They understand the Greek conception of men who violated the inscrutable will of gods; they understand the renaissance conception that a breach of the universal moral law sanctioned and set forth by God, needed to be punished. They can even endure such situations as that of Claudio and Isabella in the terrible third act of *Measure for Measure*. For that unhappy brother and sister never question the right of the arbitrary power that caused so cruel a dilemma, nor doubt the absolute validity of the virtue that is named. These two strike at each other's hearts and never at the bars of the monstrous cage that holds them prisoner. Do they not, therefore, rise almost to the dignity of symbols of that moral world in which the majority of men still live?

But it is precisely with the bars of the cage that modern tragedy is so largely and necessarily concerned. It cannot deal with guilt in the older sense. For guilt involves an absolute moral judgment. That, in its turn, involves an absolute standard. And a literally absolute standard is unthinkable without a super-human sanction. Even such a sanction, however, would leave the flexible and enlightened spirit in the lurch. For if it were not constantly self-interpretative by some method of progressive and objectively embodied revelation, its interpretation would again become a mere matter of human opinion, and the absoluteness of moral guilt would again be gravely jeopardized. Not only must God have spoken; He would need to speak anew each day. The war has overwhelmingly illustrated how infinitely alien such obvious reflections still are to the temper of humanity. We must have guilt. Else how, without utter shame, could we endure punitive prisons and gibbets and battles? Is it surprising that audiences are cold to Ibsen and Hauptmann and Galsworthy, and that good critics who are also righteous and angry men deny their plays the character of tragedy?

But the bars of the absolutist cage are not so bright and firm as they were once. The conception of unrelieved guilt and overwhelming vengeance has just played on the stage of history a part so monstrous that its very name will ring to future ages with immitigable contrition and grief. And thus in the serener realm of art the modern idea of tragedy is very sure to make its gradual appeal to the hearts of men. Guilt and punishment will be definitely banished to melodrama, where they belong. Tragedy will seek increasingly to understand our failures and our sorrows. It will excite pity for our common fate; the terror it inspires will be a terror lest we wrong our brother or violate his will, not lest we share his guilt and incur his punishment. It will seek its final note of reconciliation not by delivering another victim to an outraged God or an angry tribe, but through a profound sense of that community of human suffering which all force deepens and all freedom assuages.

A Note on Comedy

THE pleasure that men take in comedy arises from their feeling of superiority to the persons involved in the comic action. The Athenian who laughed with Aristophanes over the predicament of the hungry gods, the contemporary New Yorker who laughs over a comedian blundering into the wrong bedroom, are stirred by an identical emotion. The difference in the intellectual character of the two inheres in the nature of the stimulus by which the emotion is in each case aroused. In the former the pleasure was conditioned in a high and arduous activity of the mind; in the latter it arises from a momentary and accidental superiority of situation. High and low comedy are dependent in all ages upon the temper of the auditor whose pleasurable emotion of superiority must be awakened. He who has brought a critical attitude of mind to bear upon the institutions and the ways of men will coöperate with the creative activity of a faculty which he himself possesses and has exercised; he to whom all criticism is alien can evidently find no causes for superiority within himself and must be flattered by the sight of physical mishaps and confusions which, for the moment, are not his own. Pure comedy, in brief, and that comedy of physical intrigue which is commonly called farce, cannot from the nature of things differ in the effect they strive to produce. But they must adapt their methods of attaining this common end to the character of the spectator whose emotions they desire to touch.

It follows that pure comedy is rare. Historically we find it flourishing in small, compact, and like-minded groups: the free citizens of Athens, the fashionables of Paris and London who applauded Molière and Congreve. But in all three instances the reign of pure comedy was brief, and in the latter two precarious and artificial at best. With the loss of Athenian freedom, intrigue took the place of social and moral criticism; no later poet dared, as Aristophanes had done in *The Acharnians*, to deride warlikeless in the midst of war. In the New Comedy public affairs and moral criticism disappeared from the Attic stage. In Rome there was no audience for pure comedy. Its function was exercised by the satirists alone, precisely as a larger and nobler comic force lives in the satires of Dryden than in the plays of Congreve. Nor should it be forgotten that Molière himself derives from a tradition of farce which reaches, through its Italian origin, to Latin comedy and the New Comedy of Greece, and that the greater number of his own pieces depends for effectiveness on the accidents and complications of intrigue. When he rose above this subject matter and sought the true sources of comic power and appeal in *L'École des Femmes* and *Tartuffe,* he aroused among the un-critical a hatred which pursued him beyond the grave.

The modern theatre, which must address itself pri-marily to that bulwark of things as they are, the con-tented middle classes, is, necessarily, a bleak enough place for the spirit of comedy. These audiences will scarcely experience a pleasurable feeling of superiority at the comic exposure of their favorite delusions. Hence Shaw is not popular on the stage; a strong comic talent, like Henri Lavedan's, begins by directing its arrows at those grosser vices which its audience also abhors and then sinks into melodrama; isolated excep-tions, such as the success of Hauptmann's massive satire of bureaucratic tyranny in *The Beaver Coat,* scarcely mitigate the loneliness of comedy on the stage of our time. The comic spirit which once sought refuge in satire now seeks it in the novel—that great, inclusive form of art which can always find the single mind to which its speech is articulate.

But since men still desire to laugh in the theatre, there has arisen out of a long and complicated tradi-tion the sentimental comedy. Here the basic action is pseudo-realistic and emotional. Into it are brought, however, odd and absurd characters whose function is the same as that of Shakespeare's Fools in tragedy. They break the tension and release the pleasurable feeling of superiority. More often, however, they en-croach largely on the sentimental action, and then we

have the most popular form of theatrical entertainment among us—a reckless mixture of melodrama and
farce. And this form caters, beyond all others, to its
huge audience's will to superiority. Men and women
laugh at the fools whom they despise, at the villains
whose discomfiture vindicates their peculiar sense of
social and moral values; they laugh with the heroes in
whom those values are embodied and unfailingly triumphant.

From such facile methods pure comedy averts its
face. It, too, arouses laughter; it, too, releases the
pleasurable emotion of superiority. But it demands a
superiority that is hard won and possessed by few. It
is profoundly concerned with the intellect that has in
very truth risen above the common follies and group
delusions of mankind; it seeks its fellowship among
those who share its perceptions or are prepared to share
them. It demands not only moral and intellectual freedom in its audience; it demands a society in which
that freedom can be exercised. It cannot flourish, as
the central example of Attic comedy illustrates, except
in a polity where art and speech are free. And any one
who reflects on the shifting panorama of political institutions will realize at once how few have been the times
and places in history in which, even given a critically
minded audience, the comic dramatist could have
spoken to that audience in a public playhouse.

The immediate example in our own period is that

of Bernard Shaw. Whatever the ultimate value of his plays may be, he is to us the truest representative of the comic spirit. Some of his plays have, on occasion, quite frankly been removed from the stage by the police power; none are truly popular except in the study. The bourgeois audiences who at times witness their performance have set up between themselves and Shaw the protective fiction that he is a high-class clown. Since they cannot, in self-defense, laugh with him, they attempt to laugh at him, and thus save their pleasure and their reputation for cleverness at once. True comedy, in a word, is a test both of the inner freedom of the mind and of the outer freedom of the society in which men live. Its life has always been brief and hazardous. Nor is it likely to flourish unless the liberties of mankind are achieved in a new measure and with a new intensity. For the great comic dramatist, if he would gain the most modest success, must gather in a single theatre as many free minds in a free state as Lucian or Swift or Heine seek out and make their own in a whole generation.

On Sentimental Comedy and Melodrama

In sentimental comedy the purpose of clouds is to have a silver lining. The silver lining is carefully "planted" from the start and in the last act irradiates the visible horizon. It is a perfectly open secret; the playwright would fare ill who refused to play the game. The public will endure physical but not moral suspense. It likes to be puzzled to know how the crooked will be set straight. Indeed the crooked must not be crooked in its real being at all. The clouds must be delusions. Straightness and radiance must be seen as the normal order of the world. And this normal order must be reëstablished and rendered clear by a half-humorous, half-sentimental character of native birth. This is the hero of sentimental comedy—a rough customer, preferably, but with a heart of gold, clean, wholesome, manly, chivalrous, the sworn foe of libertines, foreigners, revolutionaries, grafters, scientists, idlers. . . .

Is there anything that unites all heroes of sentimental comedy? Perhaps it is their common conviction that virtue is a definite and simple thing, that it is not to be found among the wise and learned, that it need but be discerned to transform life, and—that it pays. A curious blending of the spirit of the Gospel

with that of the Enlightenment, of ancient sayings concerning the wisdom of the foolish with those verses in
which Edward Young declared that

> All vice is dull,
> A knave's a fool,
> And Virtue is the child of Sense.

It follows that in this art of the theatre, if in no
other, we cultivate prettiness and are afraid of beauty.
How entrancingly pretty our leading actresses are!
Miss Billie Burke has an exquisite childlikeness, Miss
Laurette Taylor a liquid pathos of expression, Miss
Elsie Janis a boyish freshness and grace. Beauty is
a thing almost from another world. It would not so
swiftly reveal itself to so many eyes. It arises from
deeper sources. It brings not only peace but also a
sword. Neither in life nor in art will prettiness burn
the topless towers of Ilion. Genius and beauty hold
a menace and a flame. Talent and prettiness delight
and soothe. One might almost achieve them oneself!
Such is, unconsciously enough, the reaction of our
wider audiences. The managers and stage directors
are equally at ease. Their ways are ways of pleasantness. Miss Burke is not fretting to play Electra, Miss
Taylor is content not to appear as Lady Macbeth, Miss
Janis dances like an elf, but she does not insist on
dancing the tarantella of Nora Helmer.

So, by a happy and tacit conspiracy, pretty plays—all sentimental comedies—are found for these pretty stars—plays in which they can wear charming clothes and have their lovely innocence of aspect safely aspersed by dark doubts. No moral discomfort will arise from such plotting. You know from the first that Miss Burke and Miss Taylor are as harmless as they are pretty. They are irremediably sweet. Beauty may dwell with guilt and bitterness and wisdom, knowing the earthly and the heavenly love. When Miss Burke and Miss Taylor let down their hair, you think of the nursery; beauty with the same gesture evokes a vision of the ancient night lit by its burning stars. A whole dramaturgy of the pretty could be derived from such reflections, and it is more than a jest to point out that on the screen actresses who approach beauty of person or expression are cast for the parts of "vampires."

If prettiness and its innocence keep our dramas from being serious, they may also be said to keep our farces from being amusing. Throughout its history—and it is a very long one—farce has aroused laughter by presenting people in absurd and uncomfortable predicaments. Into these predicaments the characters of farce fall by committing the follies and excesses to which human nature is addicted. But since on our stage human nature must be shown as not really addicted to these at all, and since pretty is as pretty does, our farces are anemic and clownish. Our actresses are

pretty and must be innocent; the men may be silly, but
their conduct must be fundamentally correct.   Thus
the eternal contents of the lower human comedy which
a Molière did not disdain are reduced to a game of
hide-and-seek adorned by slightly provocative costumes.   Our moral illusionism lies at the root of the
whole situation.   We like to think of ourselves as a
nation of kindly, proper, good-looking, romantically
virile people.   Between the mirror of the stage and
ourselves we hold up for reflection that comfortable
and sentimental dream.

* * *

Melodrama, it is commonly held, owes its character
to astute plotting and to moments of intensely heightened conflict.   The briefest observation of our stage
destroys that theory at once.   Our average melodrama
is structurally stupid.   Its continuance depends on
some trick that a clever child could see through.   At
some crucial moment a false reticence or nobility is
feigned and the action rattles ahead for want of three
words of explanation that only perversity coupled with
dullness could have withheld.   There is no nimbleness
of invention in these plays.   The plots are monotonous
and heavy; the final act is, as a rule, openly bankrupt
of ingenuity or resourcefulness.   Of this fact the audiences are not unaware.   It is possible to overhear
jesting comments on it from people of no startling intelligence.   Yet these people will go again and again, and

melodramas are—far beyond farce or sentimental comedy—the safest investments of the commercial managers.

The explanation is not far to seek. It lies in the
extreme psychical gregariousness of the average American. Spiritual isolation has no bracing quality for
him. To be in a minority makes him feel indecent to
the point of nakedness. His highest luxury is the mass
enjoyment of a tribal passion. War, hunting, and persecution are the constant diversions of the primitive
mind. And these that mind seeks in the gross mimicry
of melodrama. Violence, and especially moral violence,
is shown forth, and the audience joins vicariously in
the pursuits and triumphs of the action. Thus its hot
impulses are slaked. It sees itself righteous and erect,
and the object of its pursuit, the quarry, discomfited
or dead. For the great aim of melodrama is the kill-
ing of the villain. Whether he be tribal enemy or
moral or social dissenter, he is permitted small successes, shadowy evasions, brief exultations. But these
are known to be momentary, and felt as rudely ironic.
The net tightens, its cords cut closer and closer into
the victim's flesh until the magnificent instant of the
clicking handcuff or the whirring bullet is ripe.

Stronger and deeper is the final instinct that adds
fierceness and joy to the mimic man-hunt of melodrama. The villain, whether tribal enemy, mere for-
eigner, or rebel against the dominant order, is always

represented as an unscrupulous rake. He attacks the honor of native women, and thus—especially if his skin is a tinge darker—there is blended with the other motives of pursuit the motive of a vicarious lynching party of the orthodox kind. The melodrama of this approved pattern brings into mimic play those forces in human nature that produce mob violence in peace and mass atrocities in war. Nations addicted to physical violence of a directer and simpler kind have cultivated the arena and the bull-ring. Those, like ourselves, who desire their impulses of cruelty to seem the fruit of moral energy, substitute melodrama.

A Note on Dramatic Dialogue

DRAMATIC dialogue is of two kinds. In the older and, it has often been thought, nobler kind the dramatist lends the characters his own energy and beauty of speech and they are differentiated one from another primarily by the sentiments they utter and only secondarily, if at all, by the manner of that utterance. Stylistically the speech of Jason and Medea, Othello and Iago, Alceste and Philinte is one. Whether such dialogue be written in verse or prose does not affect the method involved. Bernard Shaw, despite an occasional use, as in certain scenes of *Major Barbara*, of the raciest vernacular, shares with his characters his own wealth of energy and eloquence and wit. Among the Neo-Romantics this stylistic unity is even more pervasive, and in Yeats and Hofmannsthal, kings and poets, ghosts and clowns use the identical forms and cadences of speech.

The second kind of dramatic dialogue, which may be called the naturalistic, makes such a selection from the actual speech of men as to produce an illusion of reality. Here the language of the characters is adjusted to their class and occupation, their actual mentality and range of expression, and individual pecul-

35

iarities of speech are studied and suggested. The occasional use of naturalistic dialogue is old. It is found in Horace's account of the bore he met on the *via sacra*, in Swift's *Genteel and Ingenious Conversations*, in one magnificent passage after another of *Tom Jones*. But its conscious cultivation as a dramatic medium is recent. That cultivation dates from Hauptmann's *Before Dawn* (1889) and the early acts of Brieux's *Blanchette* (1891). It is not found in either Augier or in Ibsen, both of whom use a kind of dialogue no less lifted into a unity of style because that style is sober and pedestrian.

The dramatist who feels an original creative impulse need not ask himself: Ought there to be a third kind of dialogue? That question has no meaning in art. He must ask himself: Can there, in the nature of things, be a third kind? If a dramatist strives, as Mr. David Liebovitz did in *John Hawthorne* the other day, to make very simple people speak, he can either lend them a heightened medium for all they would say if they could, as Arthur Symons did so beautifully in *The Harvesters*, or he can select all that is vivid, strange, and passionate in their own actual speech, as Hauptmann did so incomparably in *Rose Bernd*. But when he takes their vernacular, as Hauptmann did, and tries to use that vernacular as Symons used the medium of *The Harvesters*, he creates a confusion of styles which at once renders impossible that suspension of

disbelief which is dramatic, no less than poetic, faith.
To point out the veracity of this detail or that is futile.
He has used the true details of speech, but he has used
them in a manner that robs them of persuasiveness as
art. For art can produce nothing closer to reality than
an interpretative illusion of it. And the artist can fail
of this object with well-observed details almost as
easily as with those that have been observed ill. We
are convinced by every word that Beatrice Cenci utters;
we are equally convinced by the speech of Jones in
Galsworthy's *The Silver Box*. But Jones's vernacular
used in an attempt to produce the timeless human intensity of Beatrice would issue in feebleness and dis-
cord.

The average American playwright uses a semi-
naturalistic dialogue romanticized by a bad tradition
drawn from both plays and books. The people of Mr.
James Forbes talk as shoe-dealers and insurance agents
think they talk just after they have read their favorite
magazines. Mr. Eugene Walter once had his moments
of veracity. But, as a rule, the dialogue of popular
plays is an imitation of the speech that people like to
assign to themselves in their day-dreams, full of false
gaiety and spurious nobleness. The serious dramatist
cannot, of course, use this method. His choice is
forced upon him. His manner must be akin to Shelley's or to Galsworthy's. He will hesitate to use the
former for artistic as well as for practical reasons.

The stylicized drama, whether in prose or verse has, as a matter of hard fact, not even the sympathy of our better actors and our better audiences. The reason for this is not pertinent here. The fact remains. Hence our American dramatist is almost under the necessity of observing and making a selection from the actual speech of his contemporaries.

At this crucial point another difficulty confronts him. Cultivated Americans talk more bookishly and are more alienated from the vernacular than the corresponding class of Europeans. They use slang and common turns of speech with an ironic under-tone. The reason is that our common speech is not folk-speech, but a corrupt newspaper English filled with the ephemeral catch-words of sport and trade. An educated Irishman can talk like an Irish peasant and still talk beautifully; an educated American cannot talk like a clerk in a cigar-store without a grin. We have islands of folk-speech in New England and the South. But the sporting page of the newspapers, the Victrola record of songs sung by Nora Bayes, and the slang of the drummer are rapidly obliterating the dialects that savor of the earth. The best, then, that the dramatist can do is, probably, to follow the novelists who use the corrupt speech of the populace naturalistically but with a constant and communicated awareness of its true character. That is what Sinclair Lewis did so admirably in *Main Street*, and what Miss Zona Gale did equally well in *Miss Lulu Bett*. That both the speech in question and the author's awareness of its quality can be transferred to the stage has been amply illustrated by the first act of the dramatized version of Miss Gale's story. If the playwright, finally, desires to deal with the minority of cultivated and sophisticated Americans, he has but to turn to modern literary English, using it with what simplicity and colloquial ease he can command. And here, again, the novelists from Edith Wharton to Joseph Hergesheimer have set him excellent examples. But whatever style he uses must be used consistently and purely. Good dialogue, as Galsworthy has pointed out, must be like hand-made lace. One thread of foreign material or inharmonious color breaks the web and destroys the illusion.

A Note on Acting

CRITICISM of acting alternates, as a rule, between un-governed ecstasy and rough disdain. Whether Hazlitt celebrates the praise of Mrs. Siddons or some contemporary that of John Barrymore, what we get is the impression made by a commanding or romantic personality rather than the record of an artistic achievement. Lesser actors, on the other hand, are dismissed without a word of interpretation or instruction. Nothing in their work is clearly defined or accurately understood by the criticism they receive, and little is left them but to defy their censors and to blunder on. Yet actors deserve helpfulness and close understanding. Their artistic life is precarious and transitory. An approach to perfection before middle age is their one hope. Only so can they expect a few rich and untroubled years before the lights go out upon them and their audiences.

> Nor paint nor pencil can the actor save—
> Both art and artist have one common grave.

The matter, closely looked upon, is not forbiddingly intricate. When toward the end of his life Johnson was asked to sum up the virtues of Garrick, he said: "A true conception of character, and a natural expression of it, were his distinguished excellencies." We speak more subtly to-day and deal in finer shadings; the intimate nature of the modern drama, the withdrawal of the stage-picture into its frame, and the consequent abandoning of all declamation, have given the words "natural expression" a far intenser meaning. But to the substance of the old critics little need be added. Actors are still, as Colley Cibber declared them to be, "self-judges of nature, from whose various lights they only take their true instruction." It is when they are such that we hear, in the fine words of Lessing, "that natural music which unfailingly opens all hearts because we feel that it comes from within and shows us that art has shared in it only in so far as art and nature can become identical."

The actor's art, then, however difficult to practise is not difficult to understand. His intelligence must grasp the poet's intention and his imagination lend it the concreteness of life. But his imaginative activity must always be the servant of what he has observed in himself and others. Nature must be his teacher and his norm. He has never, to be sure, seen a Hamlet or an Iago, an Osvald or a Henschel. But he has seen men in spiritual perplexity, sardonic mirth, bleak despair, and dumb confusion. Having built up the concrete projection of a character from his imaginative observation, he must, with that personal plasticity which alone justifies his calling, melt into the being which the poet and he have combined to fashion, and speak and act and live outward from within that being's very soul. His faults may therefore be referred to a failure in one of the three basic elements of his art— intelligence, imaginative observation, plastic expression. Or else he may, yielding to a frequent temptation of powerful or peculiar personalities, abandon the art he is well fitted to practise and depend on a continuous display of his own self under this or that borrowed name.

The commonest fault of our actors to-day is a failure in the second element of their art. Their eyes are turned upon the theatre, upon some vivid personality of the stage, upon their careers and persons, upon anything except nature and its spontaneous expression amid the varying moods of life. They are not unskilful in portraying sharp moments of passionate excitement. There are few actresses who cannot weep convincingly. They have all wept and, like many modern people, involuntarily watched the adequate expression of their grief. But in the level passages of a play, in attempting to depict the life from which the passions arise, these very actresses will be of an insufferable and vulgar artificiality. They have never taken the trouble to observe themselves or others at common tasks or in quiet hours; they have no ear or eye for the kind of speech and gesture by which the subdued but important business of nine-tenths of life is carried on. They disdain nature and, rather than observe it, transfer to their private behavior the metallic graces of the stage, mouthing and languishing at home and abroad. On the stage they are passable or even eloquent when the situation is tense. But they say "good morning" or lay the cloth for breakfast with the air of pinchbeck princesses in disguise. The men are more aware of the texture of common existence. But instead of observing nature, they substitute personal mannerisms that are realistic enough but wear thin by constant and wearying repetition in play after play. Mr. Sidney Toler has a quaint glance and Mr. Wallace Eddinger an amusing aspect of hurt innocence. But since neither one has observed life, his mannerism has become a mere trick and his art an exhibition of that single possession. The personal mannerisms of Mr. Dudley Digges cannot be studied from the stalls. When we see him we lose him and dwell solely with the excellence and truth of what he has created.

The ambition of the average American actor is not to interpret drama or create character, but to be John Barrymore. In regard to Mr. Barrymore's artistic intelligence and fascinating gifts there can be no question. But as Fédya in *Redemption,* as Gianino in *The Jest,* and as Richard III he played but variations upon the theme of himself. There was the same *morbidezza,* the same sense of inferiority becoming fierceness or malign splendor, the same white profile, the same stricken grace. In each piece one became primarily aware not of a creature of a given world and kind, but of John Barrymore's somewhat hectic idealization of himself. It was not, first of all, acting, but superb daydreaming upon the stage. Mr. Lionel Barrymore, devoid of his brother's poignant charm, is a far more scrupulous practitioner of his art. His Neri in *The Jest,* was shaggy, boisterous, full of excess and gorgeous wildness; his Mouzon in *La Robe Rouge* was polished, quietly cynical, hard, and graceless in an inimitably truthful modern way. The two creations had nothing in common but his intelligence, his powers of observation, his ability to project what he had grasped and seen. The contrast illustrates this brief argument and sums it up. To emulate John Barrymore is both foolish and impossible; to imitate his brother is to have a just and fruitful notion of the actor's art.

II
The American Stage

Mr. Belasco Explains

FOR thirty-seven years Mr. David Belasco has devoted himself to the art of the theatre. In remote cities where no other American manager's name would be recognized, his is known. If a girl is applauded in amateur theatricals in Peoria or Denver she writes for counsel and help to David Belasco. There is a Belasco legend composed of anecdotes that commercial travelers swap in smoking-cars; there is a Belasco biography in two stout volumes by the late William Winter; there is, finally, issued but the other day, the word of Mr. Belasco himself.[1] The critics may jeer mildly; the knowing ones among the public may show a correct disdain. They are all impressed. A Belasco opening —the first of any given season above all—still commands its very special little alertness and thrill.

And why should not these people be impressed? Mr. Belasco's dedication to his chosen art is as tireless as it is complete. He has spared no toil and no expense to produce what he considers beautiful things. He has never been cynical about his success, but has taken it to be the reward of his hard gained merits. He is satisfied with himself and with his public. He has

[1] *The Theatre through its Stage Door.* By David Belasco.

made art pay. He still makes it pay. And who has the right to deny the unfailing qualities of every Belasco production—the silken delicacy of its surface, the unobtrusive perfection of its visible details, the gentle glow and harmony of its color schemes? Not those, assuredly, who daily applaud the less perfect productions of quite similar plays on another street. Nor those others who, in high places and humble ones, proclaim the theatrical theory of the drama—the theory, namely, that plays are "built" in the theatre, not written in solitude; that they are constructed to be gladly heard by any audience of the moment, not created to be overheard by the finer spirits of the age.

Of that theory Mr. Belasco's practice is the best of all possible illustrations. A manuscript to him is not something to be interpretatively bodied forth. It is a little raw material and a convenient starting-point. "Almost invariably," he tells us, "the exceptionally successful play is not written but re-written." During the crucial week of preliminary rehearsals, he continues, "I rewrite, transpose, change, and cut until the manuscript is so interlined that it is almost impossible to read it. . . . If it seems too heavy at a certain point, it must be lightened; if too tearful, laughter must be brought into it." It is no wonder that Mr. Belasco is the author or co-author of many of the plays he has produced, and that he has sedulously avoided the work of any master. What could he do with the method of production so truly attributed to another manager in another land, the method that strives to give to each play "its individual style, its special atmosphere, its peculiar inner music." [1] "Who am I?" asked Oscar Wilde, only half in jest, when he was urged to make changes in *An Ideal Husband* for the production of the play, "Who am I to tamper with a masterpiece?" Mr. Belasco has not tampered with masterpieces. He has left them alone. And that is what every producing manager must do who desires—as our professors counsel and indeed command—to build successful plays in the theatre.

To Mr. Belasco, at all events, the play has been but one of many things. "The all-important factor in a dramatic production," he tells us, "is the lighting of the scenes." And again: "The greatest part of my success in the theatre I attribute to my feeling for colors translated into effects of light." He has ransacked the curio shops of ancient cities for furniture and the fabled East for silken draperies and has found in these "explorations in search of stage equipment really the most interesting part" of his work. And he has sought out charming and promising young persons and chosen and adjusted them as he would select and adjust folds of rich velvet or the glow of a new tint of light into the harmony of a production. He has "made" Frances Starr and Jeanne Eagels and Lenore Ulric and Ina

[1] *Max Reinhardt.* By Siegfried Jacobsohn. Berlin. 1910.

Claire. He has fitted them like brilliant bits of glass
into the shifting colors of his successive scenes. And
yet this prestidigitator of light and shadows, this clever
artificer, this glorified interior decorator, whose consciousness has never been touched by either life or art,
holds himself to be a realist. "I am a realist," he proclaims proudly and sincerely. And he is a realist because on his stage he "will allow nothing to be built of
canvas stretched on frames. Everything must be real."
He is a realist because when he produced *The Music
Master* he "searched for people in the theatres of the
lower East Side"; because he employed real Japanese in
The Darling of the Gods and caused the Uhlans in
Marie-Odile to be represented by real Germans! In
such preoccupations he has spent a lifetime of labor and
has ended by impressing a nation. He has touched
nothing that he has not, in his own inimitable sense,
adorned.

What has he touched? He could never, as we have
seen, produce the work of a great dramatist. No great
dramatist would have endured the process. He has
given us one play by Pierre Wolff and one by Her-
mann Bahr. He saw the unfulfilled promise of Eugene
Walter and staged *The Easiest Way*. The rest is sentiment and drapery—*The Music Master* and *Du Barry*,
The Auctioneer and *The Darling of the Gods*. He ven-
tured on *Tiger, Tiger*, but accompanied it by the ultra-
saccharine *Daddies;* he re-wrote and re-built *Dark*

Rosaleen until it was pretty and trivial enough; he engaged Mr. Albert Bruning only to load him with Chinese robes in a spectacle play by George Scarborough. He likes to have children on the stage as often as possible and hence avoids plays in which there are none. For such plays, in his opinion, "view life flippantly and cynically, like the comedies of Bernard Shaw"; he is blandly unconscious of the contemporary practice of his profession elsewhere, except to fling a querulous word at Max Reinhardt, a producing manager who, during the first eight years of his career, presented one play each by Aristophanes, Euripides, Calderon, Molière, Goldoni, Lessing, Henri Becque, Tolstoi, Hauptmann, Donnay, Chekhov, Gorki, and J. M. Synge, two by Hebbel, Kleist, Gogol, Strindberg and Schnitzler, three by Grillparzer, Wilde, and Maeterlinck; four by Schiller, Goethe, Wedekind, and Hofmannsthal; five by Ibsen; six by Shaw; and nine by Shakespeare!

The Gold Diggers by Avery Hopwood is a perfect example of Mr. Belasco's art. There is a foolish little story about a savage uncle who wishes to rescue his nephew from a chorus girl and himself falls a prey to the charms of another. There is a sunny little moral about chorus girls duly emphasized by a gray-haired mother. But neither the story nor the moral is very obtrusive. These, as well as Mr. Hopwood's little local jests, serve, after all, only to call attention to a burst of morning sunlight which Nature would do well to emulate more often, to Mr. Belasco's exquisite bits of color, to the influence of his training upon the talent and personality of his latest creation, Miss Ina Claire. The latter illustrates his most solid gift. He can train actresses. Miss Claire's rendering of her lines in the first act has the daintiest verisimilitude and the nicest precision in its miniature way; her crucial scene in the second act, in which she feigns intoxication so well and yet never lets us lose a sense of spiritual delicacy, is a little marvel of its kind. But the almost total waste of talent and hard work exemplified in these bits symbolizes once more and depressingly enough the character of Mr. Belasco's whole career. Miss Claire has intelligence and flexibility; Miss Jobyna Howland has her unfailing vein of natural and robust humor; Mr. Bruce McRae is a careful artist; quite minor members of the cast do credit to Mr. Belasco's persuasive methods. Thus a highly agreeable entertainment is offered, an entertainment that eludes criticism by never coming within its proper range. But we dare neglect neither the show nor the master of the show so long as any are left among us who believe that either one sustains the slightest relation to the drama or the drama's interpretation on the stage of our time.

Four Theatre Guild Productions

I. *The Faithful*

THE Theatre Guild began its career with the presentation of a fantastic comedy, *The Bonds of Interest,* by the Spanish playwright, Jacinto Benavente. The success of that first venture was small. Next the Guild undertook to give the public the wholesome bread of realistic art, and the brilliant success of *John Ferguson* serves, even after a discounting of its adventitious elements, almost to mark an epoch in the American theatre. It is, therefore, a little disheartening to the friends of the Guild to see them, in their third production, John Masefield's *The Faithful,* return to the exploitation of the merely fantastic strain in dramatic literature. For it is a fact that the ventures of the insurgent theatre and of the art theatre in this country have constantly come to grief through their cultivation of the over-refined, the exotic, and the fanciful. From the play lists of our little theatres one would infer, if one knew no better, that the staple of the modern drama is the neo-romantic in its most tenuous and cloudy moods. It was not by such methods that the Théâtre Libre and the Verein Freie Bühne revived and re-created the European theatre. Each began by presenting those foreign plays which most searchingly interpreted the human problems of its immediate present, each saw and fulfilled its final mission by opening the theatre to the young revolutionaries of the native drama. These stages began with Ibsen and Tolstoi; they ended with Curel, Brieux, and Hauptmann.

The success of those now historic undertakings was no accidental one. It was not by mere accident that the early audiences of *The Faithful* at the Garrick Theatre felt a perceptible estrangement and chill. The Greeks were right when they made the Muses the daughters of Memory. It is from memory that the creative imagination springs. The spiritual energy of the poet may indeed transform and creatively interpret the world. But it must be a world that he has originally seen and lived in. It must be founded on a soil that has known the tread of his footsteps and the moisture of his tears. He may project the elements of his experience, as Shakespeare did in *The Tempest* and as Goethe did in the second part of *Faust,* into a region unseen by any mortal eye. But the elements of his own experience, the vision of his own mind, the pang of his own heart must still be present there. What does Mr. Masefield deeply know of the feudal life of Old Japan? What experience of his own soul has he bodied forth through that shadowy and alien world? Pictures and translated legends caught his fancy, and from these pictures and these far-off echoes in another tongue he wove a pattern of ghostly lights and mimic passions. But he has not shared these passions and the tragedy has not been, in some ultimate sense, part of the tragic life of his own heart. The old Horatian tag with its sovereign common sense sums up the whole matter:

Si vis me flere, dolendum est
Primum ipsi tibi: tum tua me infortunia laedent.

It is worth while to glance briefly at the fable of the play. By guile and force the crafty and unscrupulous daimio Kira takes possession of the narrow hills and woodlands of the daimio Asano. An envoy from the imperial court comes to that province. Partly through fear and enmity, partly because Asano will not stoop to bribery, Kira deliberately misleads him concerning the nature of the ritual by which an imperial envoy must be greeted. Asano thus becomes guilty of an involuntary sacrilege and is forced to commit hari-kiri. His exiled retainers, led by his counselor Kurano, pledge themselves to avenge the death of their lord. After devious wanderings and on the very point of abandoning their purpose in despair, their opportunity comes and they slay Kira at the moment of his highest earthly power and triumph. The trouble with all this, for a contemporary audience, arises from the fact that the remoteness of the action is not redeemed by any warmth or reality of motivation. Kurano is at no moment conscious of any essential injustice in the coil of circumstance in which he and his friend are involved. To him the matter is a purely personal one. Asano has been killed. Therefore Kira must be killed. The same is true of the humbler retainers who abandon their wives and children, not in order to bring a little more justice into their world, not to prevent such things, not to protest against tyranny through Kira's death, but simply to kill him to even the score. Nor is it true, as may conceivably be urged, that this is demanding a modern attitude of the ancient Japanese. The peasant wars of medieval Europe illustrate the dim but massive sense of general injustice that may fire humble and unlettered men.

Granting, however, the purely personal and hence remote nature of this conflict, and disregarding, for a moment, the total absence of the poet's deeper and more spontaneous energy from the execution of the play, the vexing question still remains: in what manner are these characters to behave? There is an impression current in the West that the Japanese are and, above all, historically were given to an extraordinary measure of stoical self-repression and continually sheathed their human impulses in the rigid forms of some prescribed ceremony. Mr. Masefield's central incident and the exciting cause of his whole action, being concerned with a breach of ritual, deepens that impression. But so soon as we leave that incident, we are plunged into a loud, turbulent, and yet futile violence which accompanies us to the end. What is no doubt true is that both elements, the self-repression and the violence, exist in the history and character of the Japanese people. But Mr. Masefield has not made the necessary synthesis; he has not derived both from some fundamental trait of that character. And he has not done so for the simple reason that he does not know enough. The play is not written from within the ethnic consciousness with which it deals. Sound and convincing art cannot arise from a contact so external.

The players struggle painfully with Mr. Masefield's unsolved problems. Mr. Rollo Peters, as Asano, gives an admirable performance. He is the impassive, stoical, gentle-souled Japanese aristocrat—a creature all silk and steel. He answers our preconception which is, however, quite untested by experience. Mr. Augustin Duncan has been reproved for the boisterousness of his performance as Kurano. It is true that he is noisy and jerky. But he could make out a fair case for himself by appealing to his author's text. Mr. Henry Herbert is keen as a blade and subtle as a poison in the part of Kira. But again it is our untested preconception of an Oriental villain that wins our applause. The worthlessness and indeed the danger of all such preconceptions are among the most terrible facts of our time. Hence the poet here leads us into uncertainties of judgment which are fatal to any

pleasure or any suspension of disbelief. Mr. Lee
Simonson's scenery is of a delicate beauty. Form and
color are a more universal language than articulate
speech. Only a people's speech can lead us to its soul.
Both Mr. Masefield and ourselves stand on the thresh-
old of a gate to which we have no access.

II. *Jane Clegg*

Politics crumble and opinions and moralities fade.
Life, whose meaning must somehow be sought within
itself, goes on. The tongue of the propagandist turns
to dust, but the voice of nature remains. Merely to
capture and project some bit of reality is, therefore,
to practise not only the best art but the most philosophical. Such art seems quiet enough amid the noisy
contentions of the day. But its quietude is that of a
tree amid rockets. The rockets glitter and go out; the
earth-rooted tree will shelter generations.

St. John Ervine's *Jane Clegg* is not a great play,
even though we measure in terms of depth and intensity rather than of range. But it belongs to a great
kind. Isolated plays of this kind have had a way of
being written for the modern English theatre and of
having no successors by the same hand. There was
Elizabeth Baker's *Chains* and Githa Sowerby's *Ruth-
erford and Son*. Perhaps Mr. Ervine's success in the
theatre will fortify his talent, will render it more fruitful and also more faithful to itself. And that is neces-

sary. For it is likely to be forgotten that he wrote
Jane Clegg in 1913 and *John Ferguson* two years later
and hence tended to lapse from the perfect sobriety,
the weighty reality, the strictly inherent irony of the
earlier play. In *John Ferguson* the people are real
enough, though James Cæsar verges on the monstrous
and "Clutie" John on the unsoundly fantastic. But
these people are involved in a coil of circumstance—
the mortgaged farm, the delayed remittance, the false
suspicion of murder—which smacks strongly of the
melodramatic theatre.

In *Jane Clegg* the people are found in no predicament except the inevitable one of their own natures,
and the dramatic process is identical with the exhaustive exposition of their inmost selves. With the highest skill and courage Mr. Ervine carries out the purity
of his intention to the very close of the play. Henry
Clegg leaves his home. The climax of the story, however, is not in that action but in that last talk between
himself and his wife which gives our vision of him its
final clarity and expresses his blundering justification
of his own miserable self. Thus the logic of reality is
completed and his physical departure is not an action
by which a play is closed but the symbol of a life's
necessities.

That life in which the play, despite its title, really
centers is completely unrolled before us, although the
dialogue contains little or no technical exposition in

the older sense. But we are made aware of the shab-
bily gay, irresponsible father; we see the garrulous,
foolishly indulgent mother. We know how Henry
Clegg, ignorant, awkward, rigidly respectable in his
sentiments, goaded forever by his hungry senses, has
sneaked and bragged his way through the years and
how he would have done so quite peacefully to the end
but for his wife's rectitude of mind and decision of
character. That is his catastrophe. Not the meanest
creature can exist in a state of being continually shown
up. It cannot live under so fierce a light. Some rag of
self-esteem, however falsely come by, must cover the
nakedness of every soul.

But Mr. Ervine has not missed the fact—and at this
point he touches greatness—that his cockney clerk with
a mind as stale and shabby as his very clothes and
speech is the absurd and tragi-comic battleground of
great forces. Henry Clegg does not know it, but his
civilization has made of him a man monstrously divided
against himself. Through generations it has bred into
his very bone an assent to certain moral principles and
sentiments. But it has left his nature and his instincts unexplained and untouched. Hence the whole
man is but one gesture of furtiveness. Everything
about him is false. His soul is shoddy. Truth is to
him the highest indecency. Thus when he is about to
leave his wife and go off to Canada with his "fancy"
woman, he is deeply pained and shocked at his wife's

callous willingness to let her own husband to whom
God has joined her go without wails or recriminations
or the sense of the presence of sin. He has a brief moment that verges on a grotesque self-righteousness. He
is a wretched sinner but at least he has the grace to
know it. That is his religion. Jane may be pure and
honorable. But she has no sense of sin. It almost
frightens him. In Jane, on the other hand, there is
illustrated the slow and painful struggle by which a
few people here and there learn to sweep aside the
moral convention and lay hold upon the moral fact.
Since Henry's actions and her emotional reactions have
destroyed whatever peace or beauty their marriage
ever held, how empty to go on babbling about its sanctity! It is a burden and a shame. Both she and the
children will be better off without him. She feels a
natural pang at the breach with her youth and her
heart's past. But the pang is not uncontrollable. She
turns out the gas and goes upstairs.

Thus it will be seen that the intellectual content of
the play is weighty enough. But it is never emphasized
nor abstracted from the stuff of life itself. It appears
through those traits and attitudes of the characters
which arise from the impact between the individual and
the processes of that civilization within which he has
been molded. But to grasp the simple reality, as Mr.
Ervine has here done, is enough. If the grasp be but
firm and close the universal values will appear more

strongly than if the dramatist had reflected on them first and watched life afterwards.

Mr. Reicher's production of the play for the Theatre Guild is undoubtedly the most perfect thing on our stage to-day. It has an exquisite discretion; it does not impair the fullest sense of reality at any point; it has found the beautifully right atmosphere and gesture for every moment in the play's shifting moods. It allows no sense of artificial transition from mood to mood to awaken in us, and it preserves inviolable its seamless illusion of both the continuity and the change of life. Thus the spectator need never become aware of it as of something consciously done, but can yield himself to the power of the embodied play as to an undivided artistic and spiritual experience. And that is rare. We have other good productions. But they are very consciously and proudly good, and often their excellence throws only into starker relief the hollowness of the play on which they are expended. Or else a single unsubdued and "stagy" actor shatters the illusion. The five players who are associated with Mr. Reicher in *Jane Clegg* have blended their personalities wholly with the inner life of the play. Its world has become theirs. We do not remember them except in these shapes which they have assumed. The identity of art and life is for once complete, and thus the two hours during which we watch them are a pure example of that enlargement of our contracted selves through a vicarious experience which is the very core of art itself.

III. *Jangled Lives*

As its fourth subscription performance of the season of 1920 the Guild presented Strindberg's *The Dance of Death*. The production had the two notes of faithfulness to fact and density of moral atmosphere which mark Mr. Reicher's work. The hexagonal tower-room designed by Mr. Lee Simonson for the first part of the play combined clearness and freedom with a somber and menacing beauty. The players were sincere and created occasional moments of unaffected eloquence; it is doubtful whether they had quite penetrated to the inner substance of the play. Mr. Albert Perry displayed an extraordinary virtuosity without an inner assumption of the character he portrayed. Mr. Dudley Digges, one of the best actors on our stage, is too homespun and forthright for Strindberg. Miss Helen Westley alone conveyed the sense of a vivid experience and of having projected into the play not only skill but a soul that can be troubled. Despite its comparative inadequacy, the production brings to an honorable close the second season of the only American theatre of which we can be wholly proud.

What a play! Written in 1901 it leaps beyond its year and ours and establishes the dramaturgy of the future. Its method is as astonishing as it is simple.

It deals with people, not with moral attributes. It
does not let an abstract quality overshadow a man.
Strindberg clove to the root of the ancient fallacy in
the Horatian council to "let Medea be fierce, Ino tearful, Ixion perfidious, and Orestes sad." For the result
of such characterization is to give us Ferocity, Perfidy,
Sadness. What was Othello's occupation during the
period covered by the play when he was not jealous?
Did Alceste consider the question of social probity at
breakfast? The drama is full of "humors" and "ruling passions." Rarely until very late does it present
men and women. The reply that a dramatic action
demands a concentration and an overemphatic treat-
ment of its motives only restates the old fallacy in
another form. The psychologist tells us for conven-
ience about abstract memory or imagination. In reality
there are no such things. There are indeed, in the
thumping Stevensonian phrase, "passionate crises of
existence." But they hardly arise when "duty and
inclination come nobly to the grapple." Who knows
his inclination? Will it be exactly the same if it rains
to-morrow? Suppose she wears her hair differently in
the morning, or there is a slump in the market, or one
wakes with an attack of influenza? These noble and
naked absolutes grimly face to face were all very well
when your heroes were kings or generals making grandiose and probably vicious decisions at the risk of some
one else's skin. And duty? Shall I do my duty—the

thing prescribed from without by social compacts and moral traditions, or shall I do *my* duty, a thing so difficult and fragile and much to be desired? Can either be disengaged clearly enough at a given moment to justify the eruptive gesture of the dramaturgic tradition?

The Captain and his wife in *The Dance of Death* have seen each other so long and so closely that they no longer see each other at all. They try, like all people, to find moral tags in the name of which they can justify their mutual hatred. It is a profoundly true circumstance that Alice does this more continually than her husband, who yields quite unreflectively to his vindictive impulses. The woman is more passionate, yet more desirous of justifying her hatred. Hence she is eager to prove to him the qualities that explain it. She has, no doubt, chances enough. Again and again she convinces her friend and kinsman Curt. But in the end all hatred breaks down because all isolation of moral qualities becomes impossible. We know least those whom we know best, because we see them no longer analytically but concretely. We have no clues, because every clue becomes coarse and misleading when brought to the test of a reality so intricate and obscure. This husband and this wife feign, at times with passion and terror, to despise and hate each other. Yet they are unable to break their galling chains because, having passed beyond the perception of mere evil qualities in each other and seeing each other as concrete psychical organisms, they cannot hold either contempt or hatred long enough. They shift and waver and know too much to rise to the point of willing and they die in the inextricable bonds in which they are caught.

"There are disharmonies in life," Strindberg lets Gustav say in *Creditors,* "that cannot be resolved." The tragic outcome is that there is no tragic outcome. There is no liberating action and no appeasement of the heart. The years drag on and the shadows lengthen and then comes the dance of death. Children grow up and fall into the same entanglements and almost at once the familiar disharmonies begin to sound—as Alice hears them from Judith and Alan and the lieutenant. But the will to live and continue the race gilds all beginnings with romance, and the Captain and his wife in the tower-room are neither an example nor a warning. Nor is it only the young whom instinct robs of vision. Alice has but to make the immemorial gesture and Curt, the clear-minded and the disillusioned, is in flames.

Yet from this very play there arises a hope beyond the note of compassion with which, contrary to the custom of his more acrid years, Strindberg ends his action. It is no accident that the Captain and Alice live on an island. Most married couples do. They have the same friends and see the same scenes. People and the very trees and streets take on the blurred colors of that tense

and monotonous and islanded existence. They cling
to each other and restrict each other and seek to enforce agreements and concessions and harmonies of
which the very nature must be the spontaneity of perfect freedom. They assume possession and practise
force, and the island becomes a prison. The Captain
and Alice stayed on the island as each other's keepers.
Thus each became at once a tyrant and a slave. If
only they had tried a little wandering and used their
island as a place of peace and refuge, and renounced
possession as the one hope of coming into their own
at last! No, the disharmonies cannot be resolved. But
they can be silenced. Where the hope of a rare and
difficult happiness ends, peace and freedom may begin.

IV. *Liliom*

Franz Molnar's *Liliom*—the "Roughneck"—presented by the Theatre Guild illustrates with extraordinary force and freshness the plasticity of dramatic
form. Instead of a play in three acts or four we have
here a dramatic "legend in seven scenes and a prologue." To emphasize this matter of form is to recall,
of course, the unteachableness of the human mind.
Despite the theatre of the Hindus, the Greeks, the medi-
evals, the Elizabethans, the moderns, your average
director, critic, playwright believes that the form of
the drama is now immutably fixed. He has substituted
a dead formula for a living reality and guards that

formula with belligerent ardor. Therefore to us, at this moment, the very form of *Liliom* has a special and exhilarating charm.

That form was used in a tentative way by Hauptmann in *Elga*. It was deliberately cultivated by Frank Wedekind, from whose works the Hungarian Molnar undoubtedly derives it. It seeks to substitute an inner for an outer continuity, successive crises for a single one, and to blend chronicle with culmination. It takes the crests of the waves of life as the objects of its vision. The last wave merges into the indistinguishable sea. Film technique may be said to have influenced this form or even the chronicle method of Shakespeare. But it does not select its episodes to tell a story. They must unfold the inner fate of souls. In Wedekind and the expressionists the scenes are not only symbolical from the point of view of the entire action but also in their inner character, and little attempt is made to preserve the homely colors of life. What makes *Liliom* so attractive is that Molnar has avoided this extreme. He has used the expressionist structure and rhythm; the content of his scenes is beautifully faithful to the texture of reality.

Poor Liliom, barker for a merry-go-round in an amusement park, what is he but once more the eternal outcast, wanderer, unquiet one? He hasn't been taught a trade; he can't settle down as a care-taker; he isn't canny like the excellent Berkowitz. But he loves Julie.

She weeps over his worthlessness and he strikes her—
strikes her out of misery, to flee from self-abasement,
to preserve some sort of superiority and so some liking
for himself.   She is to have a child and something
cosmic and elemental tugs at the bully's heart.   Are
love and fatherhood only for the canny ones, the tread-
ers in the mill, the hewers of wood?   This is the conflict that destroys him.   He is, viewed in another fashion, Everyman, and the little play, which has its shoddy,
sentimental patches, is a sort of gay and rough and
pitiful Divine Comedy.   Liliom did not ask to be born
with those imperious instincts into a tight, legalized,
moral world.   Society demands so much of him and
gives him nothing wherewith to fulfil those demands.
The world process has not even given him brains enough
to think himself beyond demands and restrictions.   He
struggles with his body and nerves.   His mind is docile.
He believes that he is a sinner, he doesn't doubt that
there are police courts in heaven as there are on earth,
that there are cleansing, purgatorial fires, and a last
chance, maybe, to be good.   But neither the fires of hell
nor his belief in them have power to change the essential character with which the implacable universe
brought him forth.   His notion of an expiatory action
is to steal a star from the sky for his little daughter.
He is Liliom still, and the joke is on the order with
which man has sought to snare the wild cosmos.   The
joke is on a man-made world and a man-made heaven,

because both that world and that heaven have used force. The joke is not on Julie. Julie has used love. "There are blows that don't hurt; oh, yes, there are blows that you don't feel." Love does not feel the blows. Love does not demand nor coerce nor imprison. Paradise is in the heart of love. For the sake of that ending you forgive Molnar the shoddy, sentimental little patches, for the sake of that moment which is beautiful, which is indeed great.

Among the many admirable productions of the Theatre Guild that of *Liliom* may unhesitatingly be classed first. It is of a beautiful perfection. A scrupulous respect for reality is combined in it with a strong and sober imaginative sense. The first may be attributed to the direction of Mr. Frank Reicher. He was brought up in a school where veracity was understood and practised as in no other period of theatrical history. The imaginative lift that the production has is largely due to Mr. Lee Simonson. Better than any other scenic artist among us he can convey the sense of out-of-doors, of the free air, of gardens and horizons. His spring really blooms, his autumn is russet and full of melancholy. His railroad embankment in the fourth scene is a triumph of the imaginative vision of reality, his "courtroom in the beyond" of an airy, restrained, compelling fancy.

The actors were assisted by the fact that the directors did not tamper with the play. Its folk-character is preserved and so its people retain their fine, concrete humanity. Thus, for instance, Miss Eva Le Gallienne, whose impersonations have hitherto been slight and faint and bloodless, is here transformed into a peasant girl, awkward and rude but full of the patience of a deep passion and the tenacity of a noble endurance. Mr. Joseph Schildkraut fulfilled all the expectations that were entertained of him. Once or twice he forced the note of stubborn impudence, as in his entrance into the infernal flames. But predominantly his Liliom is memorably racy, vivid, and exact. Miss Helen Westley surpasses all her recent performances in a part that demands not only harshness and verve but a bitter pathos and a wise relenting; and Mr. Dudley Digges, whose portrait of The Sparrow is a little masterpiece of sly rascality, heightens our sense of his flexibility and insight. And it would be ungrateful not to mention the no less excellent accomplishment in minor parts of Hortense Alden, Henry Travers, Edgar Stehli, and Albert Perry.

Gorki and Arthur Hopkins

WHENEVER the characters of tragedy dwell in their traditional isolation, the inner logic of the play must be sustained by ascribing their misfortunes wholly to their erring wills. But once that isolation is broken, once life comes streaming in, the cold ache of guilt yields to a brotherly community in suffering. Such is the secret of Gorki's technique and of his dramatic reasoning in *Night Lodging*. The fierce, eternal little tragedy of love and jealousy in which Michael Ivanov and Vassilisa, Natasha, and Vaska are involved does not flare in the void. Nor do the characters who surround them serve either as background or as mere choric witnesses. The coil of life is one. Gorki might have written another play about the same people and have shifted the main emphasis upon the richly indicated tragic experiences of others among them. And we are, indeed, made fully aware of the Actor's life and doom and can build up imaginatively the entire fabric of all these other lives. There are no subsidiary characters in this drama, as there are none in reality. Each soul is of supreme import to itself, and in that dim night lodging as on a larger and less shadowy scene these different selves struggle for some realization of their yearnings both in the world of things and in the minds of their fellows. Nastia and the Baron cry out in bitter pain against the unbelief that meets their romantic stories. But it is not these stories in themselves that they are concerned for; it is the communication to others of the realities of their inner lives. For only so can they mitigate the anguish of their futility and their loneliness. It was his intimate perception of such facts that led Gorki to break the traditional dramaturgic pattern. Each man is the protagonist of his own drama, and that drama, in such a world as the present, is commonly a tragic one. There is in life no such person as a "first citizen" or a "second gentleman" whose function ends when he has listened to a hero's speech. The men and women in *Night Lodging* have and sustain an intimate vision of the course of the central tragedy. But ever the cries of their own hearts break forth and silence the voices of the passions that contend around them. Individual dramas detach themselves from the general rumor of life and sink back into it. But that rumor is itself made up of an hundred dramas and we need but listen a little more steadily here and there to catch the tragic accents of each one. Hence it is clear that the flowing and wavering technique of this play is not due—as we have been and shall be glibly told—to a neglect of right craftsmanship or to unfamiliarity with the theatre, but to a closer and a juster vision of human life.

Together with the tradition of the psychical isolation of a tragic action, Gorki also abandons that of its pseudo-nobility. His people are the outcasts, the rejected and disinherited of the old Russian order. They drink and brawl and jeer. But they also sing and yearn. From all their follies and futilities, lifted above their degradation and their woe, rises the voice of their hope "for something better." Only the landlord and policeman are content, though even their satisfaction in a little power and brief authority is touched by the ferocity that springs from fear. The others, out of these lowest depths, are still striving and, like the Actor, make their final exit only when all striving seems quite vain. And they speak of the desirable not as a state of power and possession but as a state of freedom, and of human life not as of something finished and rigid but as of something that men may somehow understand and master and guide. It is the old wanderer Luka who has come very near to solving that mystery. He believes them all, because he sees beyond the words to the passions of their speech. He understands them, because his compassion has transcended all the common categories of moral judgment. He returns again and again to the wonder and strangeness, the terror and the tragic beauty of the merely human. "To be a human being—do you know what that is?" To know that fully is the deepest and the most healing wisdom. Luka is the voice of that new spirit which

Russia has brought into the modern world. We hear
it in Dostoevski as we hear it in Gorki. It can give
beauty and reality to words that would sound mawkish
on other lips. It has cast aside the moral values which
sustain the members of a merely economic or political
hierarchy in their self-esteem and their several sta-
tions and has sought man in his simple humanity, having nothing but the glow of his passions, the pain of
his heart, the aspiration of his mind. And it is this
spirit that makes *Night Lodging* a play of such consoling and, if rightly looked upon, of such cheering power.
Many spectators, including the best-known reviewer on
our daily press, have found it unbearably gloomy.
They see the shadows on the damp walls, the dusty
sunlight struggling through the dim window-panes, the
Tartar's broken arm, the vodka glasses, the poverty,
the sin. They miss prosperity and bright raiment and
easy falsehoods and fortunate love. They do not hear
the faint music of that more human world toward which
we are traveling, toward which even these outcasts had
set their still unseeing faces—that world which shall
hold all men in freedom, in which there will be left no
spot to which any can be cast out.

We owe this production, as we owed that of Tolstoi's
Redemption, to Mr. Arthur Hopkins. The mere statement constitutes, in the present condition of our commercial stage, a measure of praise and gratitude to
which nothing need be added. Nor did Mr. Hopkins

stop at selecting the play. He strove to understand it. An unfamiliar dramatic rhythm had to be expressed. The pulsing of many lives had to be indicated, the parallel but never coincident throb of many passions, the rise and submergence of the more vivid central action. All that has been more than adequately achieved. Only in the final act is one magnificent moment—the outburst of Satin—permitted to predominate a little too emphatically, and one suspects a touch of weariness on the manager's part, a slight impatience after the disappearance of Vaska from the scene. But this is a very minor blemish. The players, accustomed to the false and the flashy, literally surpass themselves. Mr. Alan Dinehart's performance is far from being the most distinguished. But when one recalls him as the singing waiter in an ephemeral farce and then sees him here, pale, troubled, brooding, impassioned, rising to true spiritual expressiveness, one is confirmed in an old suspicion that it is not the actors who dictate the impossible selections of our stage. Miss Gilda Varesi as Vassilisa is, as she should be, acrid and turbulent. But she does not fail to sound the illuminating and eloquent note of helplessness in the face of her own strong passion. Miss Pauline Lord, whose admirable art is seen far too rarely, has the grace of a wild abandon as Nastia. She beats against the invisible bars of her cage and we share the ache of her wounded heart and hands. Mr. Edward G. Robinson as Satin sulks and smolders until the word of liberation comes to him and then rises to his great moment with a fervor not less convincing for its almost lyrical touch. The Actor of Mr. Edwin Nicander is wan and subtle, broken, strangely humorous and pathetic; the Luka of Mr. W. H. Thompson is perfect in the grace of kindliness, natural wisdom, and unborrowed dignity. Thus sound art liberates the actor no less than the spectator, and truth and humanity find and restore us to our deeper selves.

A Modern Chronicle Play

It is the dramaturgic school of Scribe and Sarcey which has persuaded both the wise and the foolish that a play must be tight as a glove and orderly as a machine. But all art belongs to the biological and spiritual order and its forms are infinite in number and plasticity. There are good plays and bad ones, but none that are not plays because they fail to conform to a convention or a pattern, even as there are comely faces and ugly faces, but none that are not faces because they do not coincide with some anterior conception of beauty. Hence all technical objection to Mr. John Drinkwater's *Abraham Lincoln* may be set aside at once. It "plays." Therefore it is a play. It is a chronicle play, a "history"; it seeks to recreate the rhythm of life by methods as old as *The Life and Death of King John* and as new as Hauptmann's *Elga* and *A Ballad of Winter*. Most modern plays have returned, for the sake of verisimilitude, to the pseudo-Aristotelian unities of time and place. But most modern plays deal with single culminations in the fates of men, and these are, by their very nature, brief and strictly localized. Mr. Drinkwater has chosen to show six culminating moments in Lincoln's life, and since each of the six scenes

has its own unity of effect, its own dramatic life and
progression, and since each moves toward a point at
which historic and artistic culmination are identical,
the stodgiest technician has but an illusory reason for
his quarrel.

The strictures of the historian, who can justly charge
that the Lincoln of the play is little more than the
Lincoln of popular myth, are not to be dismissed so
easily. But they apply to the play only as a written
document. In the acted drama the intention of the
author is luminously clear. Each scene of Mr. Drinkwater's play is not only a crucial episode in the life of
Lincoln, but it is also a vision of the struggle of a great
people, through which the tragic character of all mass
conflict is symbolized for the living world. The intention of the interpretative third scene—the keystone of
this whole structure—should have escaped no one even
without the very just explanatory note which Mr.
Drinkwater has added to the bill of the play. He has
tried, as he truly points out, to lend "heightened significance to a certain strain in Lincoln's character and
to certain movements and tendencies in the human
mind that he led and directed." What is that strain
and what are those tendencies? Both may be summed
up in a brief phrase: Mercy *is* justice. The Abraham
Lincoln of the play is an uncouth, kindly, humorous
man of the people, careless of all things save his spiritual vision, tolerant in all things that do not seek to

break the essential rectitude of his mind. He knows
nothing of personal enmity, nothing of tribal hatred.
He rebukes the fierce shallowness that would humiliate
the enemy or crush him. He is stricken with horror
at the thought of war becoming a "blood-feud." His
ideal is to keep the vision inviolate without war. If
war does come, its aim shall be to defend the vision,
not to destroy the foe. He is firm when others are only
stubborn, steadfast when they are belligerent, mag-
nanimous when they are vengeful. And this symbolical portrait of him has not only, as a whole, the "imaginative lucidity" which Mr. Drinkwater claims for it,
but also a high moral value for a world stricken by the
same diseases that men were suffering from in Lincoln's day.

The chief faults in Mr. Drinkwater's execution can
be easily and briefly marked. An Englishman, writing
a play of American folk-history, he was highly conscious of the daring and difficulty of his task. Some of
this arduous self-consciousness has been communicated
to his characters. In hours of moral conflict and de-
cisive action the heat and glow of life dim the future
wholly. But Lincoln is, especially in the earlier scenes,
too aware of his historic mission and character and of
the judgment of posterity. He seems at moments to
be subtly acting up to Mr. Drinkwater's retrospective
interpretation of him. The symbolical intention thus
tends, quite often, not to irradiate the density of life,

but to disperse it. Against the resultant thinness of effect Mr. Drinkwater has sought to guard by the addition of folk-characters. But the invention of these has not been happy. The Farmer and the Storekeeper are not people, but devices of exposition; Mrs. Lincoln is not a woman, but two contradictory qualities; the maid in the Lincoln household is amusingly British. The two council-chamber scenes and the scene at Appomattox are the purest in quality of effect because they are freest of the effort to supply imaginatively what only first-hand experience can make authentic. A little history is a dangerous thing; pure poetry is truer.

The production of this play stands or falls, of course, with the ability of the actor who takes the central part. It would have been impossible to receive the impressions here recorded, had Mr. Frank McGlynn been less than adequate. And his task was a staggering one. It is difficult enough to interpret the protagonist of the ordinary biographical play under the severe and jealous eye of the historian and the specialist. But every American is, in a sense, a specialist on Lincoln. He is not only a folk-hero, but one with whom men still living walked and spoke, and who is bound to the entire present generation by an immediate and a verbal tradition. Through a single obviously false note in his performance Mr. McGlynn could have become, with fatal ease, absurd and offensive. But his performance, however incorrect historically in this detail or that, has

a final rightness and harmony of effect. It may not
convince the conscience of the scholar and the eye-
witness. It cannot offend the heart and mind of the
most fastidious beholder. Mr. McGlynn has a simple,
a humble dignity; he has gleams of quiet humor and
moments of stern enough determination. But his determination avoids the shadow of truculence; his humor
glints but on the edge of sadness; his kindliness never
sinks to the over-soft. He has the correct height and
narrowness of person. He is ungainly without being
ignoble, loose-limbed but knitted from within. If there
is a touch of the merely sentimental in his posture at
the end of the first scene, it is because the dramatist
has asked the impossible. A lank, bearded man in a
frock-coat, kneeling in prayer beside the "parlor" lamp,
recalls the conventicle and the evangelist, not the fol-
lower of Jesus and the friend of man. In the fifth
scene, on the other hand, Mr. McGlynn reaches the
highest point of his performance through silence. Lincoln spends the night propped up on chairs in Grant's
headquarters at Appomattox. To that weary figure,
grotesquely garbed, resting uneasily from so much sor-
rowful endurance, Mr. McGlynn has succeeded in giving sadness, loneliness, a grave beauty of the spirit, a
homely magnanimity, a visionary touch of the tragic
end to come. This is Lincoln as the heart of man con-
ceives him.

We have here neither a great play nor a great performance. Both seek and gain—omitting all faults and inadequacies of execution—such adventitious aids to interest and impressiveness as the highest and most enduring art avoids. The historical hero is too much enmeshed in the particular which is transitory and not sufficiently enmeshed in those concrete things which are not transitory because they have a touch of the universal fate of man. In the realm of art Hamlet and Faust are greater and truer than Napoleon or Lincoln. But to our stage of to-day *Abraham Lincoln* is bread and wine amid a glut of painted sweets and brackish water.

The Tyranny of Love

IT was on April 25, 1891, that a play called *Amoureuse* had its first performance at the Odéon in Paris. The author, Georges de Porto-Riche, who was even then forty-two years old, had contributed a one-act play, *La Chance de Françoise,* to the repertory of the Théâtre Libre three years before, and had also written a one-act play in verse. He had tried his hand at lyrical poetry but without conspicuous success. Nor did he cultivate or greatly extend the reputation which came to him immediately upon the appearance of *Amoureuse.* Neither *Le Passé* (1897) nor *Le Vieil Homme* (1911) shows any development of his mind or art. He seems himself to have been aware of the early exhaustion of his vein, for in 1898 he published his four plays under the very appropriate title *Théâtre d'Amour* and made no further attempt at dramatic composition for fourteen years. His fame, which presents every appearance of solidity and permanence, rests essentially on the three-act drama of domestic life *Amoureuse,* which was produced for the first time in English on February 28, 1921, at the Bijou Theatre under the title *The Tyranny of Love.*

The unrivaled excellence of *Amoureuse* in its own

84

field is due to two facts: it exhausts its subject; its progression and outcome are conditioned neither by technical exigencies nor by the use of moral fictions, but conform utterly to the native dictates of the human heart. It is as fresh and pertinent to-day as it was on its first appearance thirty years ago; to witness its performance is to reaffirm and re-experience in one's own mind the conviction that depth and exactness of veracity constitutes the highest beauty in literature; it touches one's memory even of *Heartbreak House* with a tinge of the over-eager and falsely pointed and sets into relief the over-consciousness and calculated symmetry even of *The Skin Game;* it makes all lesser plays seem like the trivial and childish fables they are. Its scrupulous perfection shows up their easy vulgarity.

> speciosis condere rebus
> carmina vulgatum est opus et componere simplex.

What distinguishes Porto-Riche is his insight into the curiosities of love, into the difficulties of the heart. The conflict between Dr. Étienne Fériaud and his wife Germaine is the eternal one between the man of creative temper to whom love is excitement in youth and repose in later years, and the woman to whom the satisfactions of love in the broadest sense are coextensive with the content and meaning of life. "It is they whom you jeer at," Dr. Fériaud exclaims, "it is the scientists,

the artists, and the poets who have bettered this imperfect world and made it more endurable. Doubtless
they have been bad husbands, indifferent friends, rebel-
lious sons. Does it matter? Their labors and their
dreams have strewn happiness, justice, and beauty over
the earth. They have not been kind lovers, these ego-
ists, but they have created love for those who come
after them." Germaine, however, cannot make the
distinction between a service of self for its own sake
and the service of a self that is identified with a great
cause. She is jealous of her husband's work, of his
very thoughts; she desires to contract his interests to
the preoccupations of love and reduce his activities to
the feeding of her ever-famished heart. She has her
case, which Porto-Riche permits her to state with tell-
ing eloquence. She has not had adventure and romance. Her absorbing adventure and romance are here
and now. But she makes the grave error of thinking
that adventure and romance can be pervasive elements
of life—not white days and their memories but years
and continuous presences. Her exactions first rasp and
then chill her husband. "I suffocate morally and phys-
ically," he cries out. "I must be free." She "rummages in his brain as one rummages in drawers." She
diminishes the preciousness of love by her eagerness
and the haste of her consents. She thus drives him
into a mood of supreme rebellion and disgust. Yet
from that moment and its irreparable consequences

springs for him that revenge of life itself which she predicts. Though all seems over between them, he returns. Nervous disquietude and jealousy have drawn him back. It is Germaine who utters a warning at last: "But we shall not be happy." The cry does not stir him. People are not happy. They are united by the very wounds they have inflicted on each other. Life is passion, conflict, resignation, and, at best, peace.

— No brief account can do justice to the dialogue of Porto-Riche, which combines an elegiac beauty of rhythm with entire naturalness and an inexhaustible wealth of psychological observation. Not every artist has mastered all the intricacies of an emotional or spiritual situation because he has known it well enough for effective presentation. Porto-Riche knows his situation to the most fleeting of impulses, the faintest reaction of the mind, the ultimate quiver of the nerves. He knows it so well that he transcends the second stage of insight at which the consciousness of complexity clogs the processes of art. He sees not only completely but with supreme clarity and order. To hear his dialogue is a liberal education in the character of art and the more difficult art of life.

We owe this production of *The Tyranny of Love* to the good taste and admirable courage of Mr. Henry Baron. He uses a translation of his own which is not always elegant and idiomatic but which is faithful and complete. It is a pity that he thought a superficial change of scene and nomenclature necessary. But the very superficiality of the attempt keeps it from being very annoying. The play is authentically before us. And the acting is more than adequate. Mr. Flateau is a bit sullen and heavy and Mr. Cyril Keightly not quite free from mannerism. But both have grasped their parts with great intelligence and sincerity. Miss Estelle Winwood reveals herself as an emotional actress of extraordinary genuineness, charm, and force. The success or failure of this production will give us the measure of the theatrical taste about us. For it constitutes nothing less than a first-rate interpretation of the best modern play of the entire season.

According to Sarcey

IT was during the two decades from 1870 to 1890 that Francisque Sarcey, with an amazing vigor and resourcefulness of mind, established the theory of the theatre as a mechanism, a puzzle, and a game. He abstracted his theory from the practice of Scribe and Sardou, stiffened and tightened it beyond the use of his models, and applied it to Sophocles and Shakespeare, Molière and Ibsen. This thing, he declared, was "of the theatre"; that was not. He insisted on the rigor of the game he had invented and reduced the creative art of the drama to a base, mechanic exercise. Since his theory deals exclusively with the effectiveness of one narrow variety of form and since his interest in substance and its development from within was practically nil, he kept the theatre both barren and static and richly deserved as his epitaph the severe judgment of Lanson: "Au lieu d'aider la foule à s'affranchir, il la flattait dans la médiocrité de ses goûts."

Why talk about "Papa" Sarcey to-day? Because he is with us. He is our neighbor at the playhouse, our vis-à-vis at dinner, the critic in our class-rooms and on our hearth. When Mr. Clayton Hamilton extols the technique of Pinero he talks pure Sarcey; when learned professors lecture of the scène à faire and refuse to singe their well-kept plumage on the fires of Hauptmann or Shaw, they are promulgating the same faith; when, some years ago, the National Institute of Arts and Letters elected Mr. Augustus Thomas as its president and presented to him a gold medal for "his life work in the drama"—there was old Sarcey enthroned and declared an immortal. And the tradition persists. Listen to the chatter of the playwrights on Forty-second Street. They do not create their plays in secret. They "make" them in collaboration during week-end trips to Atlantic City; their highest ambition is to bring back an article that is "well-made."

It is not difficult to account for the persistence and popularity of the theory of the "well-made" play. There are ninety-nine men who can mend a machine to one who can write a lyric; there are nine hundred and ninety-nine who can superintend the manufacture of sulphuric acid to one who can gain a new insight into the problem of matter. Ingenuity is plentiful, creative vision is rare. The theory of the "well-made" play installed the ingenious as lords of the theatre and discredited the creative energy of the great masters at the expense of their supposed craftsmanship. It opened the doors of dramatic art to the type of mind that likes to solve conundrums and disentangle puzzles and invent a new can-opener and treat the business of both literature and life with astuteness, deftness, and decorum. Successful playwrights needed now no longer to be born. Cheerful mediocrity could learn all the tricks of a smooth "facture"; the superficially observed stuff of life furnished merely the pawns for the game, the threads for the pattern, the rigid little blocks for the skilful structure. Thus arose the school of dramatic writing that marched toward its big scenes by the road of lost letters and sudden encounters and stolen weapons and overheard conversations and hidden wills and exotic inheritances, which refurbished the ancient trick of indistinguishable twins, borrowed the latest sleight-of-hand of the medium and the clairvoyant, and made Mr. Augustus Thomas the dean of American dramatists.

Mr. Thomas's new play, *Nemesis,* is the logical successor of *The Witching Hour* and *Palmy Days.* The modern drama, on both its naturalistic and neo-romantic sides, has not left him wholly untouched. He has felt a change in the times and been stirred by a gentle ambition to change with them. During two acts of *Nemesis,* even though the elderly silk-merchant and his young wife and the French sculptor are but vague and well-worn types, one is almost persuaded that Mr. Thomas is interested in some fundamental facts of human nature. But when, toward the end of the second act, the silk-merchant slyly, but in careful view of the audience, pilfers and secretes a bit of clay bearing the sculptor's finger-prints, we know that the great game

is on.   Character and fate and vision are dropped.
Now comes the triumph of ingenuity.   What will the
merchant do with the sculptor's finger-prints?   Well,
he has them transferred to rubber stamps and forces
his wife to summon the sculptor to their house.   There-
upon this gentleman of spotless life, addicted as we are
told, to the *North American Review* and the *American
Journal of Economics*, stabs the lady to death with the
calm precision of a stock-yard butcher, wipes the dagger, the table, the door-knobs with a kerchief, and carefully imprints on all these objects the finger-prints of
the sculptor.   There follows a trial scene in the Court
of General Sessions, written and produced with con-
summate imitative skill in all the external details of
reality, and a final moment outside of the Sing Sing
gates.   There is no happy ending.   And for that one
might be grateful, were it not that Mr. Thomas uses
a raw shock to the sensibilities merely to enforce his
belief that the one kind of circumstantial evidence commonly held to be incontrovertible may land an innocent
man in the electric chair.   This preoccupation of his,
creditable no doubt to the man and the citizen, is
artistically of an incurable externality.   But from the
point of view of Sarcey and the "well-made" play, it
provides his ingenuity with a bundle of new and effective devices.   For to this school of dramaturgy things
and their accidental collisions take the place of passions and their fatalities.

The reason for paying even so much attention to a negligible melodrama is the same for which we recalled the theory of Sarcey. The full hope of the American drama will not be realized until that theory and the resultant practice are far more thoroughly discredited among intelligent people than they are to-day; until it is vitally understood, despite noisy reputations both critical and theatric, that no creative mind is an ingenious mind, that no noble play is either "built" or "made" but grows in the still chambers of the watchful soul, that the school of Sarcey continues still to produce plays in which, as Musset justly remarked long ago,

l'intrigue, enlacée et roulée en feston,
Tourne comme un rébus autour d'un mirliton.

Pity and Terror

I

THE night of Monday, October 10, 1921, was a memorable one in the history both of the American stage and of the American drama. It brought us Clemence Dane's *A Bill of Divorcement*, Karl Schönherr's *Children's Tragedy*, and Arthur Richman's *Ambush*. The morning and afternoon of October 11 were far less happy moments in the progress of American dramatic criticism. The most distinguished of our evening papers observed that Schönherr's *Kindertragödie* was "not pleasant to contemplate" and that *Ambush* has a "miserable end." Another contemporary wondered, in regard to *Ambush*, whether it was necessary for the American drama "to go through the drab and dispiriting Manchester stage"; a third declared of the protagonist of that play that "nobody loves a weakling." It is clear that American criticism cannot lead or guide our creative life when it is necessary to remind its busiest and most vocal practitioners of so elementary a thing as Aristotle's remark that "we contemplate with pleasure, and with the more pleasure the more exactly they are imitated, such objects as, if real, we could not see without pain." The reviewers made a

94

great deal of the imperfect acting in Mr. Arnold Daly's
production of *The Children's Tragedy.* It was indeed
faulty enough. They made nothing of that magnificent
integrity and courage of his which returns again and
again to an attack upon our dramatic "forts of folly"
and now brought us the pure, severe, unfaltering beauty,
the dread and depth of Schönherr's little masterpiece.
But the American drama is closer to us and more important. And we have an American tragedy at last. We
have Arthur Richman's *Ambush.*

The character of tragic fatality shifts from age to
age with the shifting views that men hold concerning
the nature of the universe and their destiny in it. The
arbitrariness of the gods yields to the will and law of
God, and that, in its turn, yields to the immanent laws
of heredity and the cruelties of the social order. But
there is a third and, closely considered, an even pro-
founder because less debatable source of tragic fatality.
It is that which arises from the sheer and unfathom-
able diversities of human character as given. Here
there is no place for theoretic subtlety and the dramatic
idea cannot be invalidated by discoveries in medicine or
revolutions in society. The appeal is purely to human
experience. And if that appeal is broad and deep
enough the dramatic idea is safe amid whatever change
of doctrines or institutions may come to pass. Such is
the appeal which Mr. Richman has made. And he has
made it with a power and poignancy, an honesty of

mind, a richness of spiritual circumstance and a frugality in the use of external device that are plainly unique and plainly epoch-making in the history of the American drama.

I not only see Walter Nichols, the clerk who lives in Jersey City; I see his story, as Mr. Richman would have us see it, through Nichols's eyes. The man is not extraordinarily intelligent and not at all articulate. He thinks he is old-fashioned, and that word helps him out in a blundering way. But he is old-fashioned only as all depth and fineness and integrity seems to rawness and shallowness, and as the tempered and circumspect will must always seem to those who wreak their desires unreflectingly upon the world. Walter Nichols is in truth, as that reviewer remarked, weak. He is weak because the gods themselves, in Schiller's old saying, fight in vain against vulgarity of the soul. He is not only weak. He is purblind. He has lived with his wife Harriet for nearly twenty years and has not known her. He is, in the deeper sense, not capable of knowing her. Even at the end of the withering revelations which the action chronicles, even in the lowest depth of that abasement and despair into which she has thrust him, he does not know her from within. He is weak. The ideal kills. The mind that considers all things and weighs the issues of life delicately and distrusts brutal conclusions and fears to act because it fears that action may be an affront or a wound—that mind is weak in battling with the children of the world and is unpractical and unsuccessful and is a fool's mind according to the judgment of streets and market-places. Often, as in the case of Walter Nichols, it hesitates to resist evil because it does not recognize that evil and is overcome. But it is overcome only outwardly. In his extreme misery and shame Walter Nichols remains himself, bearing an inner witness to all he is forced to abandon.

The ruthless will that ensnares and drags him down is fitly embodied in two women, his wife and daughter. For it is true, however commonplace, that in woman volition is directer and more elementary in every direction than in man. The will of woman suffers more resignedly but also acts more relentlessly. To Harriet Nichols and to Margaret, the daughter, life has narrowed itself to the mere absence of ease and pleasure and of mean success. They repeat quite glibly and honestly the formulas of their moral order. And they try to observe—the older woman more than the younger—a certain prudence and to stay, as Mr. Richman points out with terrible irony, on this side of such degradation as may involve suffering and want. But the world is mere food for the voracity of their desires. Only because, until the last possible moment, they shield those desires behind the conventional forms of life, are they able to deceive and scheme and conquer. Had they been frank they would have been at once less ignoble and less destructive. They lie in the ambush of respectability and conventionality. The ideal threatens to balk their desires. They leap forth and destroy. Thus the dramatic idea is here identical with the very forces that make life. A play in which that identity is established is tragedy.

II

We are not moved by the remediable; we are not moved by the accidental; we are not moved by unrelieved moral ugliness. It may be urged that nothing is remediable. Absolutely speaking, that is true. At the end of every discussion of the character of a tragic action we meet the problem of choice. Though nothing is easier than to dispose of the will as a separable entity, we must still reckon with the unalterable subjective conviction which the spectator projects into the people on the stage that within some limits, however narrow, a freedom of choice exists. The perfect tragic action convinces us of the gradual obliteration of that margin of choice. In such a play as Henri Bernstein's *La Griffe* (*The Claw*), for instance, as in many plays of that particular French school, we are constantly irked by the conviction that the tragic protagonist could have arrested his ruin; that, on the playwright's own showing, there were forces present and alive within the man which we would, in his place, have summoned. That process of identification is inevitable. On it is

based the convincingness or the reverse of every imaginative representation of life. If, when we have granted
a character every inner difficulty, every natural weakness, every malevolence of fate, we still feel that given
his situation we could have rescued ourselves, the level
of the action in which he is involved falls below that
of tragedy. So soon as we instinctively interpose between the hero and his downfall a certain remedy pity
and terror flee and fatality turns into mere disaster.

What is true of the remediable is true in a far higher
degree of the accidental. In the world, which is a
world of causality, there is obviously nothing that cor-
responds to what people loosely call accident. In the
world of the representative and interpretative imagination all reasonableness and all convincingness is derived
from the artist's perfect control over the various strands
of moral and physical causality that weave the tragic
web. To resort to accident, that is, to the frankly obscure and unexplained, is to sacrifice the intellectual
seriousness of your action at once. That is why Clemence Dane's *A Bill of Divorcement* does not, despite its
earnestness and power, impress me as being of a tragic
character. It may be that after fifteen years of hopeless insanity a man can suddenly regain his reason.
But the proof of an action or event must be, as David
Hume pointed out long ago, strong in direct proportion
to its improbability. Miss Dane has not troubled to
supply that proof. That, finally, the suddenly recov-

ered man should wander into his old home on the very
Christmas day on which his wife has at last determined
to end her long solitariness, is to precipitate a tragic
crisis not from within its natural elements but from an
alien and extraneous source. Some allowance must indeed be made for the conventionalization of time and
space which the drama demands. But it is the unwise
playwright who accentuates this unavoidable artifice
by the use of festivals and anniversaries and coinci-
dences so perfect as to challenge belief at once.

The question of moral ugliness is a more subtle and
debatable one. It has little to do with any rude classification of human actions; it has little to do with the
external at all. Neither Macbeth who murders his
king repels us nor Rose Bernd who murders her child.
In each instance the dramatist has shown us the divine
humanity that transcends error and crime. When an
unrelieved moral ugliness is shown, it seems necessary
to the effects of tragedy that the author communicate
his sense of its quality to us. That is what Bernstein
so signally fails to do. We see his protagonist writhe
in the degradation of his exorbitant passions and never
glimpse a world beyond the fevered delusions in which
the man is caught. Thus the action is stained with a
spiritual sordidness which does not reside, as superficial
critics think, in poverty or dirt or meanness of occupation and station or in anything material and tangible,
but solely in the absence of those creative overtones by

which the artist persuades us of the integrity and transcendence of his own vision of things.

I have thought it more useful to offer briefly these fundamental considerations than to criticize either *A Bill of Divorcement* or *The Claw* in minuter detail, or to explain by a concrete appeal the genuinely tragic character of *The Children's Tragedy,* and of Mr. Arthur Richman's *Ambush.* What Dryden called "the grounds of criticism in tragedy" are apt to meet with no inquiry among us. The fear of setting up rules and being didactic is, indeed, the beginning of wisdom. But to harbor that fear is not to abandon the reasonable question: How does tragedy achieve its effects? And the answer is: By showing us human ills which we accept, upon a full understanding of all their causes, as inherently irremediable through such a form and tone as demonstrate the author's transcendence of that world of illusion which he delineates. When all these elements are present our pity is complete, our terror is rooted in reason, but we are elated and not depressed because the dramatist has taken us with him upon that peak of vision from which he surveys the miseries and the errors of mankind.

Susan Glaspell

I. *The Early Plays* [1]

IN the rude little auditorium of the Provincetown
Players on MacDougall Street there is an iron ring in
the wall, and a legend informs you that the ring was
designed for the tethering of Pegasus. But the winged
horse has never been seen. An occasional play might
have allured him; the acting of it would invariably
have driven him to indignant flight. For, contrary to
what one would expect, the acting of the Players has
been not only crude and unequal; it has been without
energy, without freshness, without the natural stir and
eloquence that come from within. This is the circumstance which has tended to obscure the notable talent
of Susan Glaspell. The Washington Square Players
produced *Trifles* and thus gave a wide repute to what
is by no means her best work. *Bernice,* not only her
masterpiece but one of the indisputably important
dramas of the modern English or American theatre,
was again played by the Provincetown Players with
more than their accustomed feebleness and lack of
artistic lucidity. The publication of Miss Glaspell's
collected plays at last lifts them out of the tawdriness

[1] *Plays.* By Susan Glaspell.

of their original production and lets them live by their own inherent life.

That life is strong, though it is never rich. In truth, it is thin. Only it is thin not like a wisp of straw, but like a tongue of flame. Miss Glaspell is morbidly frugal in expression, but nakedly candid in substance. There are no terrors for her in the world of thought; she thinks her way clearly and hardily through a problem and always thinks in strictly dramatic terms. But her form and, more specifically, her dialogue, have something of the helplessness and the numb pathos of the "twisted things that grow in unfavoring places" which employ her imagination. She is a dramatist, but a dramatist who is a little afraid of speech. Her dialogue is so spare that it often becomes arid; at times, as in *The Outside,* her attempt to lend a stunted utterance to her silenced creatures makes for a hopeless obscurity. The bleak farmsteads of Iowa, the stagnant villages of New England, have touched her work with penury and chill. She wants to speak out and to let her people speak out. But neither she nor they can conquer a sense that free and intimate and vigorous expression is a little shameless. To uncover one's soul seems almost like uncovering one's body. Behind Miss Glaspell's hardihood of thought hover the fear and self-torment of the Puritan. She is a modern radical and a New England school teacher; she is a woman of intrepid thought and also the cramped and aproned wife on some Iowa farm. She is a composite, and that composite is intensely American. She is never quite spontaneous and unconscious and free, never the unquestioning servant of her art. She broods and tortures herself and weighs the issues of expression.

If this view of Miss Glaspell's literary character is correct, it may seem strange upon superficial consideration that four of her seven one-act plays are comedies. But two of them, the rather trivial *Suppressed Desires* and the quite brilliant *Tickless Time,* were written in collaboration with George Cram Cook, a far less scrupulous and more ungirdled mind. Her comedy, furthermore, is never hearty. It is not the comedy of character but of ideas, or, rather, of the confusion or falseness or absurdity of ideas. *Woman's Honor* is the best example of her art in this mood. By a sound and strictly dramatic if somewhat too geometrical device, Miss Glaspell dramatizes a very searching ironic idea: a man who refuses to establish an alibi in order to save a woman's honor dies to prove her possessed of what he himself has taken and risks everything to demonstrate the existence of what has ceased to be. The one-act tragedies are more characteristic of her; they cleave deep, but they also illustrate what one might almost call her taciturnity. That is the fault of her best-known piece, *Trifles.* The theme is magnificent; it is inherently and intensely dramatic, since its very nature is culmination and crisis. But the actual speech of the play is neither sufficient nor sufficiently direct. Somewhere in every drama words must ring out. They need not ring like trumpets. The ring need not be loud, but it must be clear. Suppose in *Trifles* you do not, on the stage, catch the precise significance of the glances which the neighbor women exchange. There need have been no set speech, no false eloquence, no heightening of what these very women might easily have said in their own persons. But one aches for a word to release the dumbness, complete the crisis, and drive the tragic situation home.

The same criticism may be made, though in a lesser degree, of Miss Glaspell's single full-length play, *Bernice*. No production would be just to the very high merits of that piece which did not add several speeches to the first and third acts and give these the spiritual and dramatic clearness which the second already has. Crude people will call the play "talky." But indeed there is not quite talk enough. Nor does Miss Glaspell deal here with simple and stifled souls. That objection is the only one to be made. The modern American drama has nothing better to show than Miss Glaspell's portrait of the "glib and empty" writer whose skill was "a mask for his lack of power" and whose wife sought, even as she died, to lend him that power through the sudden impact of a supremely tragic reality. The surface of the play is delicate and hushed. But beneath the surface is the intense struggle of rending forces. Bernice is dead. The soft radiance of her spirit is still upon the house. It is still reflected in her father's ways and words. Her husband and her friend hasten to that house. And now the drama sets in, the drama that grows from Bernice's last words to her old servant. It is a dramatic action that moves and stirs and transforms. There is hardly the waving of a curtain in those quiet rooms. Yet the dying woman's words are seen to have been a creative and dramatic act. Through a bright, hard window one watches people in a house of mourning. They stand or sit and talk haltingly as people do at such times. Nothing is done. Yet everything happens—death and life and a new birth. What more can drama give?

II. *Inheritors*

While managers are returning from early spring trips to London and Paris with the manuscripts of plays ranging from Shaw to Bataille, our native drama is gathering an ever more vigorous life. The process has few observers. But all great things have had their origin in obscurity and have often become stained and stunted by contact with the world and its success. It need matter very little to Susan Glaspell whether her play *Inheritors*, which the Provincetown Players are producing, ever reaches Broadway. Nor need it affect her greatly whether the criticism of the hour approves it or not. If the history of literature, dramatic or non-dramatic, teaches us anything, it is that Broadway and its reviewers will some day be judged by their attitude to this work.

Inheritors is not, in all likelihood, a great play, as it is certainly not a perfect one. Neither was Hauptmann's *Before Dawn*. Like the latter it has too pointed an intention; unlike the latter its first act drifts rather than culminates and needs both tightening and abbreviation. But it is the first play of the American theatre in which a strong intellect and a ripe artistic nature have grasped and set forth in human terms the central tradition and most burning problem of our national life quite justly and scrupulously, equally without acrimony or compromise.

In 1879 two men occupied adjoining farms in Iowa: Silas Morton, son of the earliest pioneers from Ohio who fought Black Hawk and his red men for the land, and Felix Fejevary, a Hungarian gentleman, who has left his country and sought freedom in America after the abortive revolution of 1848. The two men were lifelong friends, and Morton, who had had but two months of schooling, absorbed from his Hungarian friend a profound sense of the liberation of culture and left the hill which the white man had wrung by force from the red to be the seat of a college that was to perpetuate the united spirits of liberty and learning. In the second act we are taken to the library of this college. The time is October, 1920. Felix Fejevary, 2nd, now chairman of the board of trustees, is in consultation with Senator Lewis of the finance committee of the State legislature. Fejevary wants an appropriation and recalls to the senator that the college has been one hundred per cent. American during the war and that the students, led by his son, have even acted as strike-breakers in a recent labor dispute. The son, Horace Fejevary, is introduced, a youth who thinks Morton College is getting socially shabby—too many foreigners!—and who is just now enraged at certain Hindu students who have plead the cause of the Indian revolutionists and quoted Lincoln in defense of their position. Senator Lewis thinks the lad a fine specimen. But, talking of appropriations, there is a certain Professor Holden who does not think that the Hindus ought to be deported, who has said that America is the traditional asylum of revolutionaries, and who seems to be a Bolshevik in other ways. Fejevary promises to take care of Holden, and the ensuing scene between these two with its searching revelation of spiritual processes, its bitter suppressions, its implication of an evil barter in values not made with hands touches a point of both dramatic truth and force which no other American playwright has yet rivaled. The ironic and tragic catastrophe is brought about by another member of the third generation, Madeline Fejevary Morton. To her mind, natural and girlish though it is, the monstrous inner contradictions of the situation are not wholly dark. It is two years after the armistice. Yet a boy chum of hers, a conscientious objector, is still in a narrow and noisome cell; the Hindu students who are to be sent to certain destruction are but following the precepts of Lincoln's second inaugural. She interferes in their behalf and proclaims in public, crudely but with the passionate emphasis of youth, the principles for which her two grandfathers founded Morton College. Her offense, under the Espionage Act, is no laughing matter. People with foreign names have got twenty years for less. Her uncle and her aunt plead with her; Holden asks her to let herself ripen for greater uses; her father's state pleads for itself. Miss Glaspell has been careful to make her neither priggish nor tempestuous. Some inner purity of soul alone prompts her to resist. Suddenly an outcast, she goes forth to face her judges and suffer her martyrdom.

No competent critic, whatever his attitude to the play's tendency, will be able to deny the power and brilliancy of Miss Glaspell's characterization. The delineation of the three Fejevarys—father, son and grandson—is masterly. Through the figures of these men she has recorded the tragic disintegration of American idealism. The second Felix remembers his father and his inheritance. But he has faced the seeming facts so long and compromised so much that he is drained dry of all conviction and sincerity. His son is an empty young snob and ruffian. With equal delicacy and penetration we are shown the three Morton generations—the slow, magnificent old pioneer, his broken son, his granddaughter Madeline whose sane yet fiery heart symbolizes the hope and the reliance of the future. Alone and pathetic among them all stands Holden, the academic wage slave who knows the truth but who has an ailing wife; who yearns to speak but who has no money laid by; a quiet man and a terrible judgment on the civilization that has shaped him.

In the second and third acts Miss Glaspell's dialogue expresses with unfailing fitness her sensitive knowledge of her characters. It has entire verisimilitude. But it has constant ironic and symbolic suppressions and correspondences and overtones. This power of creating human speech which shall be at once concrete and significant, convincing in detail and spiritually cumulative in progression, is, of course, the essential gift of the authentic dramatist. That gift Miss Glaspell always possessed in a measure; she has now brought it to a rich and effective maturity.

An Evening at the Movies

To criticize the movies may seem to have fallen low indeed. But Mr. D. W. Griffith, superman of the "photoplay," invites you with a gesture of quite regal courtesy. "Here," he seems to say, "is a thing that has little in common with your quarter show around the corner; here is, if anywhere, the unheard of and incomparable." You go and find yourself in the midst of a sufficiently intense experience of life, if not of art. All that depresses and discourages you in certain characteristic moods of your countrymen is here: the moral littleness and the physical magnificence, the intellectual sloth and the mechanical speed. The contrast that meets you is not the ancient and tragic one between grandeur and mortality; it is a quaint and new one between grandeur and silliness. But do not fancy Mr. Griffith a Barnum, a knowing fakir on an heroic scale. He creates or rather assembles his spectacles within the mood to which they are to appeal; he himself throbs and yells and hisses the villain with that vast audience which is stirred and shaken by these racing pictures as it could never be by the passion of Medea or the piteousness of Lear.

He has taken the tawdry old fable of *Way Down*

East—the betrayal, the mock marriage, the villain's downfall, the happy ending—and left it, in all essentials, precisely what it was. The written legends on the screen that interpret the action in a style of inimitably stale sugariness serve but to intensify the coarse and blundering insufficiency of the moral involved. These hectic appeals to the mob in favor of conventions as stiff as granite and as merciless as gangrene are powerfully calculated to tighten thongs that even now often cut to the very heart and to increase the already dreadful sum of social intolerance and festering pain. For in the applause of these audiences there is not only satisfaction; there is menace. Ten thousand people, an hundred thousand people, will, sooner or later, leave a theatre after this picture and go out into the world determined to make the ideals of Mr. Griffith prevail. Woe to a neighbor, a friend, a kinsman who shall choose to lead his life upon another plan! Against this propaganda poets and philosophers are as powerless as a child trying to batter down a door of oak.

They are the more powerless because the manager with a craftiness that, on this scale, has in it something grandiose, drives home his moral by the sharpest, the most intimate, the most unashamed appeals. A son dances a simple old country dance with his mother and, with a grave and tender courtesy, kisses her faded cheek. Dusk falls over two young lovers in an orchard. Apple blossoms sway in the breeze. Behind the screen well-modulated choral voices sing an old-fashioned ditty that brings back to every American those scenes of his earlier years from which no man can withhold a faint tenderness. Our youth does tug at our hearts. If the steady and disciplined mind recognizes, however austerely, the natural power of such things, consider how those unschooled characters go down before so vividly real and beautiful a presentation of them. They are ensnared by what is not the worst within them, and driven forth by their very pieties to persecute and to traduce their fellowmen. Who is so base that, having seen this picture, he will not battle for the security, the permanence, the sanctity of—well, of everything exactly as it is?

Mr. Griffith's "elaboration" of the story is purely scenic in kind. Not to praise his work in this respect would be an empty affectation. Life is here in great beauty and in great abundance. The gorgeous ball in the prologue, the barn-dance, the farm-yards, the sleigh-rides are all excellent. The directing especially in the barn-dance scene is superb. No stage manager has ever created a fuller sense of the authentic rhythm and thrill and abandon of reality. All the group scenes, indeed, are magnificently done. There is in them a union of strength and elasticity that required both insight and imagination to produce. Wherever no moral ideas intrude, wherever neither straight thinking nor clean feeling was to be done, wherever the scene has no signifi-

cance beyond its physical aspect and movement, Mr.
Griffith and his actors have both grace and power. It
follows that the picture reaches its highest point where
nature and naked physical danger are to be shown.
When the heroine's past is discovered, the squire drives
her—like Hazel Kirke—out into the storm and the
night. The scene is excessively silly and mawkish.
But he does not drive her out, remember, into a storm
of paper from the wings. It is an authentic blizzard
in the forests of Vermont. The girl flees to the frozen
Connecticut river. But the ice cracks and is riven and,
lying on a floe, she is driven toward the thundering
falls. The hero follows her and saves her at the last
moment. A shabby old trick! But the feigning is reduced to a minimum. A large engineering staff worked
for two months to force nature itself to enact this scene.
The whirling storm, the icy water, the racing floes are
actually there. It is not art, but it is magnificent.

Anthropologists tell us that in primitive society the
violator of a taboo is the central object of vengeance.
Yet when trained observers question members of the
tribe as to the reason for any particular taboo, primitive man cannot even comprehend the nature of that
question. His whole concern is with the how, never
with the why of his tribal customs. In the foreground
of his consciousness is always the will, never the reason.
In the face of nature he is agile, skilful, and intrepid;
before the uses of his tribe or phratry he is a shivering

and unthinking slave. The parallel is, at least, instructive. Mr. Griffith and his kind harness rivers and play with storms in order to tell the tribe what it already most potently believes, and to fortify its already overactive and perilously blind volitions. In this vicarious affirmation of its will the audience feels something that approaches ecstasy, as it also does in witnessing the contest between men and the primordial forces of the earth.

There are secondary sources of pleasure. Miss Gish is an extremely gifted young woman. The art of reproducing the exact gesture and facial expression of life could not well go further. She was present in a box on this first showing of the picture and received a deserved ovation. Yet were she to act the part of Nora Helmer, as she so exquisitely could, these audiences would turn from her in hot and angry contempt. Her art, as such, is nothing to them. They only know that she violated no taboo.

The One-Act Play in America

IN the stricter technical sense the one-act play, like the short story, is a modern invention. And even more than the short story do its restrictions demand a very high concentration of material and an economy of means so strict that its besetting danger is a spurious and loud effectiveness. But since precisely such effectiveness appeals strongly to the nerves of the average audience, the most successful one-act plays, those of Sudermann or of Alfred Sutro, have not always been the best of their kind. Strindberg's eerie acuteness of vision and Schnitzler's beautiful awareness of the dramatic life in hushed and muffled things have made the one-act plays of these two the best in the world. Such symbolical projections of a poet's highly personal sense of awe and mystery and spiritual values as Maeterlinck's *Intérieur* or Hofmannsthal's *Der Tor und der Tod* are lyrical in method, though dramatic in form, and hardly enter the question of the one-act play in the broader life of the theatre. There are isolated masterpieces such as Synge's *Riders to the Sea*. Generally speaking, however, the contemporary one-act play will conform to one of the three types: the artificial, the psychological, the symbolist.

The narrow means and tentative beginnings of the experimental stages in America have made the one-act play important in the recent history of our theatre. Nowhere else has it held a quite comparable place. On the Continent cycles of one-act plays by a distinguished dramatist are presented whenever one has chosen that form of expression. Among us there has been a cult of the one-act play as such. In the hands of the Washington Square players this cult reached its highest point. To-day, though it still persists, it is less intense. Our insurgent theatre is entering upon a robuster phase of its life. A bill of one-act plays by different authors, chosen partly to harmonize and partly to contrast, is after all a source of somewhat frail and artificial pleasure. The audiences, at all events, have commonly been a trifle self-conscious and have worn their sophistication with more pride than grace.

During the past ten years, however, the production of one-act plays in this country has been very large. It is a pity that one cannot also call it rich. But it did not need Miss Mayorga's extremely useful though somewhat fantastically edited volume[1] to tell us that rich is the one word with which to sum up all the qualities that the movement lacked. It was a movement which every one who cared for the theatre supported and still supports. But if his sanity was quite firm, or if he

---

[1] *Representative One Act Plays by American Authors.* Selected by Margaret Gardner Mayorga.

was in close touch with other things in the modern
drama, he could never lose a sense of being in an artistic atmosphere that was supposed to be keen but was
only thin. It was astir with a bustle of aspiration. But
the gusts were quick and a bit too explosive and died
down in a little mist of staleness. The figure halts.
And one is indeed embarrassed, in any critical description of these plays, by one's cordial sense of the talents
and ambitions of certain immediate contemporaries and
by one's clear vision of the lack that unites them all.
Realists or romantics, sociological or poetic playwrights,
they are all deficient in vitality, strength and sap. The
formula according to which all but three of the twenty-
five plays in Miss Mayorga's volume seem to have been
written is this: The one-act play is an admirable vehicle
for advanced thought or delicate fancy or dramatic
episode. Let us seek such a thought, fancy, or incident,
use the approved methods, and offer the result to a
little theatre. Nowhere is there a sense of that impassioned fusion of impulse and form which alone makes
art; nowhere any evidence of the fire and compulsion
of an inner experience. The exceptions are painfully
few; two or three things by Eugene O'Neil, Theodore
Dreiser's *The Girl in the Coffin*, Bosworth Crocker's
The Last Straw. These few are tragic and dramatic
not only in gesture but in feeling; they were not written to be played but played because they had been
written.

The symbolical plays are the most bloodless. They are either obviously and woodenly made, like Mr. Percy MacKaye's *Sam Average,* or ineffectually and conventionally idealistic like Miss Hortense Flexner's *Voices* or Miss Alice Gerstenberg's *Beyond.* The ideals are too correct, the sentiments too acceptable. Here is the central weakness. What these pieces lack is not skill or adroitness or good intentions. There is no free and self-sustaining personality behind them. The young Maeterlinck, Hofmannsthal, and Yeats had a vision unseen but by them, incommunicable except through their words. They had no philosophical notions in particular, no ideals for practice, no saws for conduct. But they had a personal vision of the mystery of life which burned away all other vision, darkened for the hour all other light, opened new vistas into the land of the soul. Without that there is no art, no literature, no drama. The day of the folk-singer is over. Nothing can justify the creative act to-day, as Gourmont eloquently pointed out, but personal vision. And that requires character, not in the current sense of technical blamelessness or an assent to common standards, but in the higher sense of daring to experience in order to transmute experience into ripeness, wisdom, beauty. The moral, for there is one, is this: Our young writers have been too much concerned with technique and too little concerned with their minds. The wide dissemination of technical instruction has persuaded persons to write plays whose inner equipment sufficed for a family letter. The published plays of the Harvard Workshop display the same emptiness and technical dexterity as the greater number of Miss Mayorga's exhibits. And here again the kinship of the one-act play with the short story is plain. Its composition has been taught. If it were more profitable, courses would soon appear in the curriculums of the correspondence schools. But the patter about learning one's craft does not apply to literature. What truly destined "maker" was ever silenced for lack of craftsmanship? True matter creates form. The only discipline the writer needs is self-discipline. His impulse must be like love or prayer. It is resistless or it is nothing. But how many of these contemporary one-act plays could have been left unwritten without causing their authors a moment's discomfort? That question both judges them and points the way.

The Lonely Classics

I. *Medea*

No one should fail to see the *Medea* of Mr. and Mrs.
Maurice Browne. The play reaches you with unex-
pected intensity and force. You forget that it is ven-
erable. The passion of it pounds like the sea on rocks.
Gone are the two thousand three hundred and fifty-one
years since the drama's first performance at Athens.
You find yourself face to face with Euripides, the earliest master of the problem play, the discoverer of the
great psychological dilemmas of mankind, the father
of a mighty progeny. That being so, one's little quar-
rels with Mr. Maurice Browne's production do not
greatly matter. What one missed was spaciousness
and simplicity of effect. The lighting devices are too
clever. Yet at the crucial moment they fail and the
sun-chariot is paltry. It was inevitable, of course, that
the version of Gilbert Murray should be used, and
hence the choruses—admirably chanted and spoken—
often sweep away the Euripidean passion and philosophy and transport one to Swinburne's Forsaken Garden by the brink of his mother, the sea. But Miss
Ellen Van Volkenburg acts with as compact and un-

swerving an inner conviction as if she were indeed the first prophetic proclaimer of the wrongs of her sex.

For such Medea is. When she has said that she would rather thrice maintain herself in an embattled field than bear once the pangs of childbirth she has opened the great feminist case and destroyed the legend of the sheltered woman. She also states with a hard and final clearness the injustice of woman's social dependence on her husband and stamps divorce as useless so long as the practice involves a reproach. Under the pressure of wrongs that are indeed intolerable she lends a voice to the unhappy race of woman. With her own hands she once slew her brother for Jason's sake; for him she gave up home and friends and memories; she bore him two men children. And now he would wed the young daughter of Creon—perhaps from ambition, perhaps from desire—and make Medea, to use the naked bitterness of her own words, "a thing mocked at." Why should she not be implacable? Even if today we must dismiss the murder of her children from the world of fact, we are still shaken by her passion, which even at its extreme is scarcely more cruel than her wrongs.

No wonder that Jason, accomplished sophist though he be, shrinks and withers beneath her scorn. Nor is it surprising that from a contemporary American performance he emerges as morally loathsome. We may deprecate the ferocity of Medea's deeds; we approve that of her passion. But Euripides, whom none can accuse of a lack of justice to her, has not left Jason wholly without extenuation or defense. He lets the man make three points. It was love, it was an elemental infatuation, that caused Medea to slay Absyrtes and Pelias for his sake. For the deeds done under the sting of so selfish a passion Medea deserves no reward. His guilt lay, of course, in accepting the benefit of her crimes. His second point is that no Grecian, that is, no civilized woman, would have been capable of them and that hence the Colchian murderess and sorceress—whatever her wrongs—is but continuing her ghastly career. His third point is that Medea exaggerates those wrongs monstrously because, like all women, she identifies the life of sex with life's totality. If their marriage is blest they want for nothing else; if it is unblest they become furies and lose all sense of human values.

Euripides dwells on the barbaric character of the Colchian princess. Yet through the words of Jason he generalizes from her and, ardent feminist though he is, shows his knowledge of woman's fatal nearness to the elemental and primitive. Jason balances many things in his mind; Medea does not. In their last terrible interview he reflects and remembers and regrets. She scorns to answer and appeals to Zeus. Over the very bodies of her murdered boys no doubt afflicts her. Her revenge is for her as absolute in quality as was her wrong. She sees nothing above or beyond her sense of outrage and promptly identifies it with the outraged justice of God. Therefore the score is rightly evened and a final satisfaction is hers: "I love my pains so that thou laugh no more!"

One wonders whether Euripides saw in his imagination the latter years of this tragic pair. Medea went to the land of Erectheus. There she ordained festivals and rites to make due atonement for the guilt of having slain her children. Since she believed such atonement possible, nothing ever shook her conviction that she was the purely tragic victim of a wicked man on whom she had avenged not her wrongs only but those of womankind. She cultivated an air of grandeur and of noble melancholy. She became a privileged character at the court of Ægeus and nursed a tragic and self-righteous pride. Jason had no such inner comforts. He was quite broken. But an inner break brings thought and wandering meditation. The sophist had already begun to pass from the mere acts of persuasion to deeper reasoning concerning the true character of men and women and of their harsh contentions. In the dust of a roadside he became, perhaps, more acceptable to the understanding gods than Medea at the court of a king.

Is it to consider too curiously to consider so? Assuredly there are hints in the text of the play that Euripides was not unaware of what it must have been to be married to Medea. She had made terrific sacrifices and she was fiercely faithful. But past sacrifices do not fill to-day with pleasantness or make it easier to live. Medea, like many women, was acutely conscious of them. They made her stern, superior, and exacting. Fidelity, given and received as a matter of course, is beautiful. But it is a tender and a delicate thing. Emphasized and psychically exploited it may become first a burden and then a nuisance. Imagine, to descend to the plain bread of life, a woman who plays noble variations on this theme: You must not cross me because I once slew men for your sake, and your slightest thought must be mine because mine is yours! Jason dares not tell her the truth. But the reasons he pleads for his new marriage are hollow and specious. His insincerity is evident. What he wanted was brightness and naïveness and a wife who did not bring a moral menace and austere compulsions to his bed and board. Only when Medea is in her unapproachable chariot does he tell her that real opinion of her character and her past which sent him wooing to King Creon's house. Is that ignoble as an interpretation? Then so is life ignoble. It shows the depths within depths of the great Attic poet. It points the way, perhaps, to another tragedy on the immortal legend, to *A Modern Medea.*

II. *A Human Hamlet*

Four fluted columns of olive-tinged gray with invisible capitals stretch in a semi-circle across the stage. About these the dun draperies change and melt gently into shape after shape, marking the rooms and halls and galleries of Elsinore. The abundant beauty of shifting color is furnished wholly by the costumes of the players. The columns remain even in the churchyard scene when between the two central ones there opens a vista of tumbled headstones, of an immemorial Celtic cross, and of two solemn poplars against a pallid sky. This whole imaginary world has a beauty that is full of sadness, a sadness almost eerie with the presage of imminent decay. It is shown us in the guise it must have assumed to Hamlet's vision. For his home had always been a prison to him, though like many prisons it was not without tender memories. But the scene of those memories had been darkened by haunting shapes and in the corridors of the castle there sounded the dull echo of the tread of doom.

The Hamlet of Mr. E. H. Sothern's impersonation who moves amid these scenes has achieved a final escape from the remoteness and confusion into which the problem-mongers had driven him. He is free at last of all false eloquence, all posturing, all undue consciousness of self. He is a young poet, probably a minor poet with more temperament than power. His posi-

tion and the feebleness of his impulse have kept him
from a complete dedication to his studies and his art;
but his culture is fine and a trifle sophisticated and even
at thirty he prides himself a little upon his superiority
to the rude and physical manners of the Danish court.
He had always been lonely there. He admired and
loved his father. But he idealized him too completely
ever to have known him well. The queen was not
without the natural instincts of a mother, but she was
restless, passionate, and perverse. So the little lad had
played with the court jester in the melancholy castle
gardens. But the jester soon died and Hamlet did not
find friends until many years had passed. Then he
clung to Horatio and perhaps to one or two others
with all the peculiar tenderness of a romantic and solitary soul. He became a scholar, a wit, and something
of a poet. His intellectual faculties grew sharp and
mature. But his heart remained the sensitive and astonished heart of a child. He loved Ophelia with a
frank tenderness unschooled by wisdom or experience.
His cynicism, after the manner of intellectual youth,
was all verbal and at second hand. In his innermost
soul he held the world, at least his world, to be as gentle, as humane, as proud, as pure as himself.

Then his world crumbled. His father died. His
mother's marriage wounded his delicacy to the quick.
His first impulse was to take refuge in the studious
cloisters of Wittenberg. But his fate was upon him and

there is a forlorn pathos in Mr. Sothern's quiet rendition of the line:

> "Indeed, indeed, sirs, but this troubles me."

The full horrors sweep down upon him. But Hamlet cannot at once grasp and deal with the enormity of a world so changed and ruined. The habit of long years drives him into the refuge of reticence and silence, and the naturalness of the impulse which bade him suddenly exclude Marcellus and even Horatio from his confidence is beautifully interpreted by Mr. Sothern as arising from the inherent necessities of his nature. He determines to feign madness, which is but another escape for a sensitive soul intolerably wrought upon. Yet the feigning is only for moments. Even in those moments, as during the scene with Polonius, it is tinged by his old irony. He cannot help dropping the mask even before Rosencranz and Guildenstern. And in the great scenes with Ophelia and his mother his cry is that of the stricken idealist who will not endure love in a world where it can lend itself to such uses, nor touch a mother's hand that has been so unspeakably defiled. That is his tragedy, the tragedy of a pure soul whose moral world has been riven beyond mending. He cannot set it right. Traditions and the natural passions counsel revenge. But what will revenge avail? He falls into the profound disillusion of his utterances in the churchyard—old truths that have come home to him and that are so at variance with his great praise of man—and into the recklessness of his own safety that ends his troubled and irreparably broken life.

Such is the character and such the story which Mr. Sothern projects upon the stage. He has lost all consciousness of his audience and all consciousness of himself as in the act of playing a part so famous and difficult. His Hamlet has a virile intellect and a subtle one, but a nature that is all gentleness, courtesy, kindness, and truth. Above all, he is simple at heart. The monologues as Mr. Sothern renders them lose their last tinge of rhetoric. They are impassioned or reflective self-communings, broken by the natural pauses and gestures of a man who is alone with his own soul. In the more intellectual and colloquial passages, such as the prose scene with the players, Mr. Sothern speaks as a man among men. Here Hamlet was bent upon his proper business. But it is the same Hamlet, though driven into a world of thought and action so alien and abhorrent, who uses the subtlety of his mind to confound the courtiers and who becomes his mother's accuser and her reluctant judge. It is in these transitions from mood to mood that Mr. Sothern employs all the delicacy and ripeness of his art. Beneath the irony, the wit, the bitterness, the throttling passions that drive him almost to the verge of madness, there is always heard the deeper ground note of Hamlet's innermost nature—a note of spiritual gentleness and native peace. It is this note that Shakespeare sounds again with such incomparably simple loveliness in those all but final words:

> "Absent thee from felicity a while,
> And in this harsh world draw thy breath in pain
> To tell my story"—

words that mark fitly to every intelligence and every heart the passing of the "sweet prince" of Horatio's last salutation.

Among the details of Mr. Sothern's technique it is to be remarked that he speaks the verse as verse and yet as authentic human speech. He conveys an impression of complete naturalness while never slurring the iambic pattern of his text. He uses his voice throughout like a man speaking out his insistent thoughts and not, as Shakespearean actors with fine voices are tempted to do, like a musical instrument. His diction is beautifully clear without being over elaborate. One may merely regret that he sticks to the ugly and foolish old habit of improperly sounding the "y" in "my" and "myself." His admirable realism should not have stopped at so annoying a trifle. In his movements and gestures he has equally heeded his author's warning concerning the modesty of nature. He strikes no poses, his mantle falls into no statuesque folds. He gestures very little with his arms, but his hands have the fevered motions of a highly nervous nature under great emotional stress. In brief, his performance is so refreshing and important because it lends to a character which the centuries have overladen with curious thoughts and with the dust of perished mannerisms and traditions a living validity so complete and a reality so immediate that, to one spectator at least, he revived the music of a great poem that had fallen a little silent amid the many noises of life, and brought that almost legendary figure back again into the gloom and glory of the human earth.

III. *The Life and Death of Richard III*

From the third part of *King Henry VI* and from *King Richard III* a skilled and sensitive hand has shaped a biographical play in three acts and sixteen scenes concerning the life and death of Richard of Gloucester. For this drama Mr. Robert Edmond Jones has built scenery of a dark and naked magnificence. His Tower of London blends the architectural reality with all one's imaginative visions of a harsh, bloody, and turbulent age. The throne room is rich and beautiful, but its very lines and patterns accord with the swift and cruel fate of these transitory kings.

Through these scenes John Barrymore, clad in varying bursts of color, limps as Richard of Gloucester— slow, sinister, almost feeble, hiding yet accentuating the deformities that have so wrought upon his soul.

He wears an orange doublet that glows more brilliantly for the glossy sable of his hose; wrapped in a scarlet cloak he sits on a white horse between the dark robes of a cardinal and the gray wall of the Tower; he flashes in a suit of golden armor. His face is like a dagger—now glittering, now dull. It sheathes its malevolence or strikes out. But there is this strange and unearthly thing about its temper: it breaks but it does not melt. The art of Mr. Barrymore, which is eager and self-conscious and flexible, has not been able to mold into the flowing curves of life the rigid medieval psychology of his hero. He has striven toward that end, but the result is only a gorgeous artifice.

He begins upon a note of tragic self-pity:

> Then, since the heavens have shaped my body so,
> Let hell make crook'd my mind to answer it.

It is, in his rendering, the cry of a wounded spirit that would, like his Gianetto in Benelli's *Jest*, build a protective armor about its own infirmity—there more of craft, here of ruthlessness. And he lets Richard rise to a very modern cry of self-justification in the words "I am myself alone." But at once this interpretation conflicts with the medieval ethical conventions of the Shakespeare of 1593. A cripple stung to monstrous deeds by his own sensitiveness would be aware of his own inner qualities; his conflict would not have left him without a presentiment of the relative aspect of

the moral life. Shakespeare, of course, cared little for
that. Richard is villain through and through. He
knows that the murdered Edward was a good man and
that he is a plain doer of evil "whose all not equals
Edward's moiety." He does not play with shadings or
excuses. So Mr. Barrymore, to give continuity to his
conception, lends Richard a mordant and cynical humor in whose very wildness and excess there is a hint
of the old pain. And the text does, indeed, fully bear
out the sinister humor, as in Gloucester's

> Cannot a plain man live and think no harm?

or in his swift baiting of Margaret, or in the answer
to his mother's question "Art thou my son?"

> Ay, I thank God, my father, and yourself.

But in the text this humor is like the sparks struck
from a flint; it neither hides nor betrays a malady of
the soul. It is a part of what Richard himself calls
his "naked villainy" which, for mere effectiveness, he
clothes

> With old, odd ends stolen out of holy writ.

Throughout the whole of what is, in this representation, the third act, Mr. Barrymore lets Richard show
a disintegration of the spirit that is expressed by a

growing feebleness and feverishness of speech and
bodily gesture. It was, obviously, his only refuge from
his author. For again the text plays him false. Richard is broken by danger from without and by defeat
in the field. The ghosts of his murdered men and
women are ghosts risen from a medieval purgatory to
blast and damn him. They are not the crystallization
of a long and suppressed spiritual agony. They do
not symbolize his conscience; they awaken it. Mr.
Barrymore's Richard has a tragedy of the inner life;
Shakespeare's chronicle illustrates the fact that even
the cleverest and strongest scoundrel is punished in
the end. In the tent scene on Bosworth field Mr. Barrymore has a rich and resonant moment in the awaken-
ing from that fearful sleep. But in this very moment
he is forced to belie his own conception wholly. For
his Richard, stung to excess and crime by the bitterness of fate, would have found pity for himself within
himself; his conscience would have used those "several
thousand tongues" before, or else he would have sought
to transcend it and would have hurled his defiance
against the very ministers of doom. The medieval
villain, having determined upon his course, dispensed
with conscience until hell and vengeance found him out.
Not a medieval villain of flesh and blood, of course,
who being human was divided and tormented, but the
villain of the medieval Christian tradition whom the
young Shakespeare accepted in all but the customary

inhumanity and in the customary unashamed homiletic intention.

The performance, despite the discrepancy between its own central motivation and the Shakespearean text, is an arresting and even a fascinating one. But it is not really great. Mr. Barrymore has moments of the highest histrionic effectiveness; he allures and dazzles. But the word histrionic with all its connotations stands between him and the spirit from which greatness issues. He misses here, as he missed in Tolstoi's *Redemption,* the note of an ultimate sincerity. He does not lose himself; he is not consumed in the flame of his own creative imagination. We watch John Barrymore doing marvelous things, and he watches himself with an eager appreciation and applause. He permits himself to be surrounded, notably here, by large companies of very inferior actors who play in subdued tones, raise his personality into an immoderate relief, and shatter the drama which he feigns to interpret. One quality only his Richard adds to those with which we are already familiar in him. His diction is wholly beautiful—clear, scholarly, and eloquent. He has, evidently, the finest rhythmic sense. The verses of *Richard III* do not yet flow in massive and interlinked paragraphs as in the later Shakespeare. Many of them are end-stopped and so a little hard and stiff. Mr. Barrymore observes the versification very scrupulously and yet **wrings from the lines their utmost of musical value.**

As a declamation, in the best sense, his performance is therefore beyond praise. As acting, it suffers from a display of personal idiosyncrasy and untempered power.

IV. *Macbeth in the Void*

The production of *Macbeth* by Mr. Arthur Hopkins, Mr. Robert Edmond Jones, and Mr. Lionel Barrymore raises an old and fundamental question. Neither an uninstructed dislike nor a sophisticated approbation touch it at all. When Mr. Hopkins declared that he and his associates had left behind "all compromise with realism," he flung that essential question nakedly at us and anyone moderately familiar with certain artistic tendencies of the day could have foretold the result. The mimetic function of art was to be reduced to a minimum. Mr. Jones himself could not have dreamed that it would quite cease from activity. Our eeriest and wildest imaginings still draw their elements from experience. His jagged boards cut by pointed arches have their ultimate origin in medieval architecture; the masks of his weird sisters derive, after all, from the lineaments of the human face. The imagination cannot work in the void, and abstract beauty is a contradiction in terms. What is the utmost, then, that the artist can do? He can strip art of one element of concreteness after another; he can get to an irreducible minimum; he can take this irreducible minimum and "stylicize" it. Thus he can get as far from realism as possible and land straight in a hard and shallow formalism. For these irreducible symbols have an ugly tendency to become as constant and as rigid as hieroglyphics. The rococo period also stripped life in art and shut up the residuum in symbols and substituted for the rough and beautiful multiformity of the world the gardens of Watteau and the meads of Pope.

The perfectly sincere intention of such an unwillingness to compromise with reality is to raise art to a higher significance, to omit everything that is not packed with meaning, to make a play, for instance, as Mr. Hopkins put it, "a play of all times and all people." But in this train of speculation there is involved a false analogy. If it were possible to drain art so wholly of the concrete and the fluctuating as to universalize its meaning in that bleak and literal sense, it would cease to be art and become mathematics. An algebraic formula expresses an exact and universal truth. But it is not a truth that will make the pulse quicken; it is not a truth that can be touched with hands. This ultra-symbolism may, with the utmost sobriety, be said to be flying into the face of Providence. Man is no abstract spirit. To make him typical is to traduce him. Nor is he merely clothed in his flesh and his world. He is embodied so and only so. He and his world interpenetrate each other. To tear

the two asunder is to maim both beyond healing, and
to rob both of significance by obliterating their essential characters. There can be nothing in art which
was not first in life. Hence art is significant in proportion to the richness of its vital content in terms of
flesh and gear and grass and stones and winds. Stick
to the elemental, if you choose. Nakedness can be
great, but not symbolic swathings about a core of noth-
ingness. Life has an atmosphere which art can project. Abstract atmosphere does not exist. The most
entrancing fragrance is still the fragrance of some
earthly object. Particles of its material substance detach themselves and thud faintly against the olfactory
nerve. We cannot smell anything unless there is something to smell. We cannot feel anything from art unless art is the expression of life in a concrete, recog-
nizable embodiment.

This is no plea for historical accuracy or creeping
correctness or a pedantic adherence to the Shakespearean text. It was, for instance, quite legitimate to divide
Macbeth into three moral episodes centering respec-
tively in the murder scene, the banquet-hall scene, and
the sleep-walking scene. It was, indeed, a high and
sensitive intelligence that set the play to this spiritual
and artistic rhythm. But those scenes themselves with
their heavy and monotonous coloring, their cubist lum-
ber, their asymetrical polygons and lathe triangles, are
dreary beyond measure. And they are dreary not be-

cause they mean only the essential but because, from the nature of things, they can mean nothing at all. At the end of the banquet-hall scene there is a single moment of human forlornness and of mortal ache. That moment could be felt because here, at least, candles burned and tables bore pewter cups and there arose the semblance of a habitation of man. But that image fades once more from the eye and the mind and Lady Macbeth falters, holding a pathetically real little lamp, among decorations so meaningless, because so unrelated to reality, that all the pity of her distracted soul cannot shield our nerves from the assault of the boat-like hulks in the foreground.

The final and supreme oddity of this production is that Macbeth, the "man possessed" of Mr. Hopkins's explanation, is impersonated by Mr. Lionel Barrymore as a creature of no tragic austerity, no vision of fatality, no splendor, and no gloom. He is rough, sordid, unintelligent, ignoble. He is not a hero caught in the toils of fate; he is a beast in a trap. The husky voice, the lumbering movement, the shifty vision, the tangled beard, the feeble exultation and ferocity all combine to project the idea of a common, heavy, spiritually soggy man who never approached the stature of his fate. Perhaps this is a legitimate interpretation of the murderous Scotch thane who, according to Holinshed, was always known to be "somewhat cruell of nature." Nor is it to be denied that Mr. Barrymore carries out his conception with an unrelenting consistency. But what conceivable relation could such a conception of Macbeth have been thought to sustain to the mystical abstractions which employed the mind of Mr. Hopkins and the eye of Mr. Jones? Miss Julia Arthur's Lady Macbeth, though feeble and subdued, does not, at least, wrench herself out of the frame of these eerie pictures and bring the whole decorative scheme tumbling down. Of the entire production, then, the final word must be that the best and strongest forces in our living theatre, that fine intelligence and something not unlike genius, have been wasted here for the want of some close and scrupulous reflection on the character and the possibilities of the artistic process itself. One's consolation is that those forces are actually with us and that a single mistake cannot greatly enfeeble or diminish them.

V. *The Beggar's Opera*

Spence's anecdote of how Swift once observed to Gay "what an odd, pretty sort of thing a Newgate Pastoral might make," how *The Beggar's Opera* came to be written, and how Congreve, having read the manuscript, remarked that "it would either take greatly or be damned confoundedly," is a commonplace of a hundred classrooms. It is also known that the piece did take greatly, that it made Rich the manager gay, and Gay the author rich, that the actress who took the part of Polly married an earl, and that Hogarth painted the whole triumphant company. But the opera itself drifted into gradual forgetfulness. The early nineteenth century revivals were bowdlerized, softened, and sweetened. Johnson, to be sure, had said: "I do not believe that any man was ever made a rogue by being present at its representation." But he had afterwards added in order to give, Boswell tells us, a heavy stroke, that "there is in it such a labefactation of all principles as may be injurious to morality." The "labefactation" theory prevailed on both sides of the Atlantic. In America, moreover, if we are to believe Hazlitt, "this sterling satire was hooted off the stage," because the Americans "have no such state of matters as it describes before their eyes and have no conception of anything but what they see." Virtue or ignorance, in brief, robbed the English-speaking stage for over a century of this strong, witty, and delightful work.

Its very character came to be a matter of dispute. It is, first of all, a dramatic satire in the exact taste of the eighteenth century. To ascribe to highwaymen and women of the town the pseudo-noble sentiments and swelling speech which courtly life had borrowed from the pastoral tradition was obviously amusing to a fashionable audience of 1728. That audience was also, in its own way, politically minded and relished the secondary intention by at once identifying Peachum and Lockit with Walpole and Townshend. So much for the satiric substance. It was the form of *The Beg-*

gar's Opera that made it an unmistakable burlesque of the Italian opera. Whenever the action touches emotion the characters drop speech and express themselves in sudden arias. This was the technique of every opera before Gluck and remains customary in the cruder type of operetta to this day. Contemporary witnesses are quite clear on this point. The Companion of the Playhouse asserted that *The Beggar's Opera* overthrew for a time the Italian opera, "that Dagon of the Nobility and Gentry, who has so long seduced them to idolatry." A final bit of evidence that has not always been given its due weight is the fact that the Italian opera company managed by Handel and Bononcini failed in the very year of Gay's success.

The London production of Mr. Nigel Playfair which Mr. Arthur Hopkins has brought to America gives us *The Beggar's Opera* in a form as close to the original as our modern lack of leisure permits. The satire now reaches us with all its cold, sardonic force. It is brilliantly gay, but with a cruel sort of gaiety. The Duke of Argyle in his box on that first night of January 29, 1728, was quite sure that the play "would do." He was equally sure that all rogues ought to be hanged and that to make game of them before hanging was vastly good sport. The reprieve given to MacHeath at the last moment does not soften the inner tone which the piece shares with the comedy of Congreve. This high-spirited mercilessness was no doubt in part a literary convention. But such conventions answer to a prevalent mood. To-day that mood can be accepted as a purely artistic one within which there live such incomparable verve and grace, elegance and wit. The verses are as hard but also as translucent as clear agate; the satiric thrusts in the dialogue glitter like rapiers and glide home. We are very fine fellows to-day and transcend the age of Anne in all our thinking. But we have not its magnificent perfection of literary skill, its power of sheer writing on little things or great. Our musical comedy lyrists do not compose verses like Gay; no pamphlet on the Irish question rivals the *Drapier's Letters* of Swift.

There remains the music, which will appeal more strongly to modern audiences than the wit or action of the fable. The airs were all, in their origin, folk-tunes, and students of popular song complain that the transcriptions were not faithful and that the rhythm and the whole modal character was changed. The lover of music who is not a specialist need not regret this. It was the age of Handel, a march from whose opera *Rinaldo* (1711) is actually introduced. To the modern ear the airs seem all to melt into the mood and pattern of the music of that age, to share its lovely and pure simplicity of melodic line, its clear and sober gravity, its compact and finite charm. This music is as innocent as the gods. It knows neither regret nor yearning. It is not always, not even generally, gay

But the sadness never cries or rebels. It accepts and expresses itself as a plain fact like any other. The melodies are neither like homeless souls nor like gardens in the rain; they are like Grecian urns set in the cool shadow of a well-trimmed tree. The dances are as grave and graceful as the tunes, and but for the secondary matter of decorative skill the earliest of all musical comedies may still be said to be also the best.

III
Contemporaries

The French Theatre of To-day

IT is a tradition of the French theatre to conquer the
world. The classics of the seventeenth century ruled
the stages of Europe until the coming of Lessing and
of the Romantic age. In the nineteenth century the
playwrights of France once more took possession of
the theatre. But that second conquest was wholly different from the first. The classics of the great age
summed up and embodied the living ideal of every neo-
classicist in the world. They achieved what all desired
to attempt. They were copied through an inner conviction. But romanticism destroyed the continuous
surface of European culture. It left literature concrete
in substance and national in temper. Sardou and Scribe
swept across Europe not because they expressed an
ideal, but because they expressed none whatever. Their
plays could gleam for a moment in any climate because
they were rooted in no soil. With Augier and the
younger Dumas French drama almost attained another
European hour in the older and nobler sense. But
soon the society plays derived from the works of these
two became a by-word. When finally France created
a modern drama of her own, the business of dramatic
exportation fell off. The masterpieces of her new the-

atre—*Les Corbeaux, Amoureuse, Les Fossiles, Connais-toi, Le Pardon, Amants, Les Hannetons*—though far more universal because far more concrete, have stayed at home. Yet the average theatre-goer bases his vague and simple faith in the supremacy of the French stage not upon these plays of which he has never heard, but on the persistence of the French skill of manufacturing for export the trade-goods of the theatre—Bisson's *Mme. X.*, Bernstein's *Thief*, and the books of Revues and musical comedies. These products are analogous to others for which milliners have invented the dreadful word "Frenchy."

The trouble with Mr. Frank Wadleigh Chandler's useful and very learned book, *The Contemporary Drama of France*,[1] is its light-hearted neglect of such distinctions. He has read one thousand plays by two hundred and thirty authors. He gives as much space to Bernstein as to Hervieu and almost as much to Bataille as to Curel. He thinks that brassy melodrama *Le Marquis de Priola* "sternly tragic," and finds room for synopses of hundreds of plays which, to use his own description of *Le Voleur*, afford "no criticism of life" and are "even highly improbable." Then why dwell on such a play? Because "as a bit of clever dramaturgy it has rarely been excelled." On the same principle Kistemaeckers is described as "a master of stage-

[1] *The Contemporary Drama of France.* By Frank Wadleigh Chandler.

craft." Mr. Chandler, in a word, exhibits that blank
awe which strikes so many admirable academic minds
among us at the mere sight of a hollow technical dexterity. The truth is, of course, that these masters of
stagecraft do not enter the history of the drama except
as background, contrasts, or curiosities, any more than
the versifiers of the "smart" or comic press enter the
history of poetry. All of these people may be regarded
as clever craftsmen. All understand the application
of technical processes to their particular ends. But ask
poets or painters whether, in the memorable word of
Lemaître, these craftsmen "exist" and come within the
limits of criticism at all. Our professors of literature
must, somehow, be persuaded to draw nearer to the
living practice of the arts whose progress they would
chronicle.

But to anyone familiar with its subject, Mr. Chandler's busy heaping of synopsis on synopsis and of
name on name confirms the massive impression that the
French drama has fallen upon evil days. Not one of
the younger men shares the beautiful eloquence of
Porto-Riche, the elegiac grace of Donnay, the high
seriousness of Hervieu, or even the brilliant rhetorical
fecundity of Rostand. Nor is there any creative ex-
perimentation within the art of the theatre. The old,
rigid, mechanical technique prevails. And since that
technique cannot be used without a rearrangement of
the material of life guided solely by the exigencies of

external effectiveness, the monotony of the subject matter is overwhelming. The human triangles pass before us in an unending procession. Slight variations are infinite, the foundations and essential reactions are the same. There is indulgence, there is renunciation. But both seem mere gestures and quite rigid, and the richness and the burning tragedy of life are far to seek. The World War did not destroy the triangle. The triangle simply went to war. Bernstein wrote *L'Élevation* and Bataille *L'Amazon,* and the lovers who err or were about to err are uplifted by sacrifice. They go and sin no more, while the offended spouses exhaust themselves with nobility and forgiveness and faith to the immortal dead. It is the very rhetoric of the emotions—false and metallic. One turns, with warm relief, to the more natural and Gallic gusto and gaiety of Feydeau's *On purge Bébé* and *Mais n'te promène donc pas toute nue!*

The great spirits and the great artists of modern France—the sage and stylist Anatole France, the novelist and humanitarian Romain Rolland, the poet Henri de Régnier—have stood aloof from the theatre of their country. For that theatre is, despite exceptions and interludes, the theatre of the boulevards, harsh, shallow, and turbulent. It has not followed the sober veracity of Henri Becque; it has, uninfluenced by the repeated attempts of gifted poets, found no home within itself for the realities of the soul. To succeed in it has been, commonly, to be corrupted by it. There is Henri

Bataille. He commenced his literary career as a poet and wrote *La Chambre blanche*. The verses are of an exquisite spiritual delicacy and are full of the strange loveliness and twilight glimmer that common things and experiences take on in the imagination of childhood and adolescence. Their music is soft and wavering as the notes of a violin heard across fields at dusk. Then he turned to the stage, and, after tentative plays of a poetic character, produced *L'Enchantement, Le Masque,* and the widely discussed *Maman Colibri.* The dreary adulteries of dreary people had become his sole preoccupation. And these characters do not come into conflict with society or the state or others in the pursuit of inner freedom or at the urge of any creative force. Hence the final act can never end with an inherent triumph or defeat, but must always be built about some shocking absurdity of plot or motivation. It is precisely the glib craftsmanship of which Mr. Chandler makes so much that is responsible for such a condition of the drama. The French playwrights neither dominate nor re-create the stage to their uses. They serve it and are ensnared by its supposed conventions and laws. Not till they have destroyed it will they make it live.

The German Theatre of To-day

THERE is a saying current in Vienna now: two places are crowded—the graveyards and the theatres. It is true of all the German-speaking countries. Their theatre has survived a disastrous war; it is surviving despair and bitter famine. And it does so because for many years and to many thousands it has been a source of neither mere amusement nor mere instruction but, as expression and liberation, an integral part of the life process itself. In a typical theatrical season before the war we find Sudermann, to be sure, leading all living playwrights with 1,344 performances. But Shakespeare surpasses him with 1,484 and Schiller with 1,381. Hauptmann leads the great moderns with 800 performances and Ibsen follows him with 600. Plays by Goethe, Lessing, Kleist, Grillparzer, Hebbel, Björnson, Hartleben, and Dreyer total far over 2,000 performances. And that theatre was then and is now guided and interpreted by a criticism of high and, at times, almost perverse severity. The reviewers on the chief daily papers—Eloesser, Weitbrecht, Kerr, Bab—watch themselves with jealous strictness. The luxury of a concession to the flabby or the false is unknown.

In a recent volume, full of a somber intellectual energy to the brim, Julius Bab[1] chronicles the chief happenings on the German stage from 1911 to 1919. These years mark, primarily, the passing of naturalism. Halbe and Hirschfeld continued to write, but their inner development had ceased. Hauptmann, long drawing closer to the poet within himself, became a master and leader of the youngest generation. Schnitzler and Schönherr, to both of whom Bab is less than just, wrote plays in their characteristic moods which had never been those of the consistent naturalists of the North. But the early neo-romantics who, influenced by Maeterlinck and the Viennese lyrists, led the first revolt against naturalism, faded in their turn. Or all but one. For in *Ariadne auf Naxos* the vision of Hofmannsthal deepened and his verse gained clarity without losing richness or magic. Among the older men who kept their position firmly and whose works the unquiet youth of these fateful years held to be, in a more intimate sense, its own, was Herbert Eulenberg, the poetic psychologist of doom and of excessive passion, and the cold, perverse, essentially uncreative Frank Wedekind.

The exact character of Wedekind's power over the younger generation can be best observed in the plays of Carl Sternheim and Georg Kaiser. Both have richer

[1] *Der Wille zum Drama.* Von Julius Bab. Berlin: Oesterheld und Compagnie.

natures. But what Wedekind taught them was how
to attain dramatic range through speed. He broke up
the dramatic continuity which he considered as but
productive of a futile illusion and sought sweep, variety, and also concentration by lifting his characters at
crucial and frankly isolated moments out of the darkness into a strong and sudden light. Within these apparently random scenes hurled on the stage he likewise
makes no effort to produce an illusion of reality. All
gestures become symbols; all speech races toward its
ultimate significance. A terrible yet hopeless avidness
after the meaning of life dominates this drama, and
under its cold cynicism you feel a stifled moan of pain.
There is, for instance, Georg Kaiser's *Von Morgens
bis Mitternachts*. It was successfully produced last
winter by Reinhardt in Berlin; the production of an
English version by Ashley Dukes is promised by the
Incorporated Stage Society of London. A woman's
perfume stirs a middle-aged bank cashier out of the
lethargy of his life. He steals sixty-thousand marks.
In snowy fields he meets Death and makes a compact
for a day's grace. He glances into his home to con-
firm within himself the conviction of its death in life.
He goes to seek ecstasy, fulfilment, liberation. At a
great automobile race the crowd seems to soar beyond
itself. But His Highness appears, the national anthem
is sung, and the crowd withers into a herd. The cashier drifts to a public hall and finds no ecstasy of the

flesh but sodden barter and sale. He seeks "the infinite liberation from slavery and from reward" at a meeting of the Salvation Army and meets chafferers over shop-worn emotions. He races to the black cross stitched on coarse hangings in that hall and shoots himself. "His moaning sputters forth an *Ecce,* his last breath gurgles a *Homo.*" He is a martyr to the meaningless monotony, the commonness, and slavery of life.

The "Expressionisten" share the speed technique of Wedekind, Sternheim, and Kaiser. But they seek to present man solely in terms of his inner conflicts. Only the protagonist exists. The other characters, as in Wilhelm Hasenclever's important and influential *Der Sohn,* are but his subjective visions of reality which, streaming back upon himself, determine his fate. A kindlier interpretation of life, and one less stripped of actual things and circumstances, is offered by Wilhelm Schmidtbonn; a nobler one, in the older sense, by the admirable but pathetically futile neo-classicists Paul Ernst and Wilhelm von Scholz. A little apart from these movements, yet honored within them all, stands Gerhart Hauptmann, whose *Winterballade* seeks in an old Swedish legend the inner meaning of human sin and atonement, whose *Der weisse Heiland* and *Indipohdi* summon Prospero from the land of death and dream to lament over a ruined world.

The serious German war plays are all anti-war plays. Carl Hauptmann's *Krieg,* written before the outbreak

of the conflict, predicts the destruction of human nobility and goodness through the nature of war itself;
Stefan Zweig's *Jeremias* gives voice to the grief and
despair of those thousands of Germans whose imaginative insight and human feeling isolated them amid the
tribal orgies of 1914; Hans Franck's *Freie Knechte* exhibits the tragedy of the enslavement wrought by war
upon man among the peasants of the Northern coast;
Julius Maria Becker's passion play, *Das letzte Gericht*,
tears asunder the delusion that war is part of the inherent fate of man and not a product of the murderous
greed of a few for power; Fritz von Unruh, a Junker
and a Prussian officer, embodies in the turbid passion
of *Ein Geschlecht* an unsurpassable horror of the self-
laceration of mankind.

The war plays have already faded a little from view.
Neither Kaiser nor Schmidtbonn nor Zweig is of the
stature of the men in the generation that came before
theirs.   But what still distinguishes the German theatre is its unfailing sense of the identity of art and life.
All reputable dramatists write to project the sense of
life that is in them—the passion and the vision that
must, somehow, be uttered.   Hence they insist that the
physical theatre be their servant and not their master,
and they have the coöperation of the leading managers
in all the cities of Germany.   Criticism accepts every
technical innovation and simply asks whether it served

the dramatic intention involved. Thus the art of the theatre is here a plastic and infinitely expressive one. It arises from a hunger and addresses itself to a need of the soul of man.

Shaw: Height and Decline

I. *"Impavidum Ferient Ruinæ"* [1]

MR. H. L. MENCKEN in his sagacious *Prefaces* announces the discovery that Bernard Shaw is a purveyor of platitudes. What Mr. Mencken really means is that the ripe and disciplined intelligence of a tragically small minority has achieved some sort of contemporaneousness with Shaw's thinking and lacks only his articulateness. One wonders, nevertheless, whether Mr. Mencken has descended often enough from his dwelling place of intellectual aloofness and scorn to listen to the ordinary talk of people admittedly not illiterate on, let us say, the war, or the economic problems of the world, or art, or morals. It is not the least among the great qualities of Bernard Shaw that he knows what the world is like, that his has never been a fugitive and cloistered virtue, that he has never slunk out of the dust and heat of the race. And hence the evil days that have come upon us and that have tarnished so many escutcheons of the spirit have found him erect and incorruptible, the master of himself and of his mind. What one discerns, above all, in *Heartbreak*

[1] *Heartbreak House, Great Catherine and Playlets of the War.* By Bernard Shaw.

House is the rare and consoling vision of that just man of the Roman poet whom, tenacious of his purpose, neither the fury of citizens demanding evil things nor the countenance of a menacing tyrant has power to shake in his well-founded mind.

"All great truths," Shaw announces, "begin as blasphemies." He proceeds to utter in his own person the brave, necessary blasphemies of the moment concerning the delirium of war, the vulgar attack on Germany's share in the spiritual life of mankind, the true nature of the unspeakable peace. Truths of a more startling but also of a more permanent character he presents as having been arrived at through the living experience of people in the grip of the historic process. There is O'Flaherty, the Irish V. C., who dared not tell his mother that he was fighting with the English. "She says," he confides to the local squire and pillar of the Empire, "all the English generals is Irish. . . . She says we're the lost tribes of the house of Israel and the chosen people of God." The squire is puzzled and outraged. But O'Flaherty has, to all appearances, the soft answer that turneth away wrath: "Yes, sir, she's pig-headed and obstinate; there's no doubt about it. She's like the English; they think there's no one like themselves. It's the same with the Germans, though they're educated and ought to know better. You'll never have a quiet world till you knock the patriotism out of the human race." There is Annajanska, the

Bolshevik empress in the exuberant intellectual farce of that name. Into the hopeless muddle of political authoritarians, vacillating between the orthodox sources of power, a king and a majority, she flings her electric perception of that reality from which she derives her right to act: "Some energetic and capable minority must always be in power. Well, I am on the side of the energetic minority whose principles I agree with. The Revolution is as cruel as we were, but its aims are my aims. Therefore I stand for the Revolution."

Heartbreak House was written before the war. It is the longest as well as the most important play in this volume. It is softer in tone than many of Shaw's plays; it is, for him, extraordinarily symbolistic in fable and structure; it has a touch of weariness under the un-flagging energy of its execution. He had seen, more clearly perhaps than any other European, the ines-capable shipwreck ahead. He saw a society divided between "barbarism and Capua" in which "power and culture were in separate compartments." "Are we," asks the half-mythical Captain Shotover, "are we to be kept forever in the mud by these hogs to whom the universe is nothing but a machine for greasing their bristles and filling their snouts?" His children and their friends played at love and art and even at theo-ries of social reconstruction. Meanwhile the ship of state drifted. "The captain is in his bunk," Shotover

declares further on, "drinking bottled ditch-water, and
the crew is gambling in the forecastle." "We sit here
talking," another character remarks, "and leave everything to Mangan [the capitalistic swindler] and to
chance and to the devil." It is precisely the same reproach against pre-war Europe that Andreas Latzko expresses with such ringing intensity in *The Judgment of
Peace*. Shaw prophetically represents the great catastrophe as breaking in its most vivid and terrible form
upon Heartbreak House. In the result of the symbolical air-raid he sounds a note of fine and lasting hope.
The "two burglars, the two practical men of business"
are blown to atoms. So is the parsonage. "The poor
clergyman will have to get a new house." There is left
the patient idealist who pities the poor fellows in the
Zeppelin because they are driven toward death by the
same evil forces; there are left those among the loi-
terers in Heartbreak House who are capable of a purg-
ing experience and a revolution of the soul. Thus
before the war Shaw hoped against hope that after the
days of the great upheaval of the world "the numskull"
would not win. The playlets of the war itself are the
records of his bitter disillusion. He remembers that
Shakespeare compared man to an angry ape, that Swift
rebuked the Yahoo with the superior virtues of the
horse; and he sees an army that went forth to "destroy
the militarism of Zabern" busy in Cologne "imprison-

ing every German who does not salute a British offi-cer"; and sees the victors, their swelling moral phrases unsilenced, "starving the enemies who had thrown down their arms."

It is not to be expected that *Heartbreak House* will add to its author's fame and influence to-day. The peo-ple who admired his incisive thinking and his brilliant speech when both could be safely taken as fire-works in the void will not easily forgive his rending the veils of all their protective delusions. We shall be told, we are already being told, with a cunning and useful shirking of the issues, that Shaw is less of a playwright than ever, that these plays will not "play" (care being taken not to make the experiment), and that, at best, he is the easy jester shaking the negligible bells upon his pointed cap. The truth is, of course, that Shaw is a great comic dramatist who has, at times, followed the classical methods of comedy by confronting shams with realities, man's fraudulent gestures with his hid-den self, but who, at other times, has invented the new method of presenting on the stage a battle of those naked ideas that struggle for mastery in the minds of men. His best plays quiver with dramatic life and play superbly before audiences who have risen to a per-ception of the overwhelming reality of their conflicts. To the supporters of melodrama and sentimental com-edy they are meaningless. But what, in the whole world of art and thought, is not? *Heartbreak House*

will not, it is possible, ultimately rank with Shaw's
best work; it is worthy of all that is most memorable
in his mind and art.

II. *Shaw Among the Mystics* [1]

Bernard Shaw is sixty-five and in despair. The mad
peace finished what the mad war had begun. We still
live in a state of "boyish, cinema-fed romanticism";
we are governed by grown-up children and defectives.
Strongly and naturally the doubt arises "whether the
human animal, as he exists at present, is capable of
solving the social problems raised by his own aggrega-
tion." So the human animal must be changed; we
must transform the biological process from a process
to a weapon and a tool. We must harness the Life
Force, the *élan vital*, to our chariots and drive into a
city of God which we ourselves have built. It is sheer
mysticism; and that Shaw, like the aged Comte, has
become a mystic is something like a tragic disaster. He
accepts the full position of the mystic and glories in it.
"When a man tells you that you are a product of Circumstantial Selection solely, you cannot finally dis-
prove it. You can only tell him out of the depth of
your inner consciousness that he is a fool and a liar."
Alas, that sort of inner consciousness has borne witness

---

[1] *Back to Methuselah. A Metabiological Pentateuch.* By Bernard Shaw.

to a flat earth and a wheeling sun, to virgin births and to transubstantiation, to the special creation of species, to the righteousness of human slavery and war and persecution. It is our old friend faith, the evidence of things unseen. It is beautiful and pathetic. But it has been the source of untold errors and miseries when not strictly limited to the forever unseeable. If the Neo-Darwinians are right, Shaw exclaims, "only fools and rascals could bear to live." That is what the bishops told Huxley; it is the cry of every timid sentimentalist whose world will not conform to his vision of what it should be. And this from Bernard Shaw!

He builds his mystical structure upon a basis of apparently scientific reasoning. According to the modern followers of Lamarck, "organisms changed because they wanted to," and the chief factor in the transmutation of species was use and disuse. According to the followers of Darwin, the same process is accounted for by natural selection, that is, by the propagation of a species through those individuals which are best adapted to survive in a given environment. Shaw identifies the use and disuse of the Neo-Lamarckians with Schopenhauer's Will, with his own Life Force, with Bergson's *élan vital*, with the Holy Ghost. He plays ducks and drakes with the distinction between inherited and acquired biological characters and declares that creative evolution, "the genuinely scientific religion," means literally that we can shape the evolutionary process to

our liking as we go along. The human animal will
change when it wills to change.

How should it will to change? First in the direction
of longevity. We die before experience has ripened
into wisdom. We do not attain vision and so muddle
intolerably the affairs of the world. If we lived three
hundred years we would, at least, transcend the lower
delusions of mortality. What these delusions include
no close student of Shaw can doubt. That magnificent
intellect has always been a little disembodied. His as-
ceticism is icy and his fastidiousness not quite human.
He regards sex as a nuisance and art as a bauble. He
is offended not only by disorder and dirt; he is offended
by the processes of procreation and metabolism. In a
word, he hates the body. If he is something of a superman in clarity and fire of mental vision, he is also a
super-Puritan in his anxiety to burn away the world
and the flesh in the flames of that visionary fire. The
three-hundred-year-old sages are not his goal. They
are still born of woman and nourished by the fruits of
the earth. Nor do the eerie, sleepless Ancients of the
three-hundredth century satisfy him except through
their ultimate aspirations. "But the day will come
when there will be no people, only thought." On that
day the goal will be reached—"the goal of redemption
from the flesh to the vortex freed from matter, to the
whirlpool in pure intelligence." There is no variable-
ness nor shadow of turning in Bernard Shaw. Relent-

lessly he follows the logic of his own nature. It takes him to the "vast edges drear and naked shingles of the world." But he does not stop. He has no eyes for the green earth or its poor, passionate, struggling inhabitants. He whirs his iron wings and sets out on his lonely quest into the intense inane.

The five dramatic books of the revelation of the new vitalist religion are less brilliant than Shaw's earlier works, less humanly sagacious in detail, and, despite several bravura passages, less eloquent. But they have all his old energy and rapidity of intellectual movement and the last two, *The Tragedy of an Elderly Gentleman* and *As Far as Thought Can Reach,* are matchless exercises of a cold imaginative vigor building its structures out into the void. Yet so divorced from essential human feeling are these stupendous parables and legends that Shaw never suspects, for instance, the true character of his Ancients. He means them to inspire awe; they arouse pity and disgust like the Struldbrugs of Swift. Did he, by any chance, remember his great predecessor and draw the parallel? Swift, having castigated the follies and the crimes of mankind, holds up as a saving ideal the simplest goodness, gentleness, and innocence of soul. Shaw, suaver in gesture but in reality more terrible, finds no hope in any quality of human nature. It must be transcended; it must be obliterated; it must be remembered with loathing and contempt. Man must return "to the whirlpool

in pure force" whence the world arose. Form itself
has become an ache to Shaw. He thirsts for nothing-
ness. He destroys the cosmos not like Faust with an
imprecation, but with an argument. In no sense will
mankind take his bleak parable to heart. It is the
monument of a great despair. But men do not despair.
They are sustained by the very things that Shaw holds
to be negligible if not noxious—by love and art, food
and wine, and even by a little warmth when, after darkness, the goodly sun returns.

The Quiet Truth [1]

Good manners are commonly associated with a safe disposition; a gentleman with well-creased trousers and a nice taste in cravats is not suspected of a bomb under his coat. Comfortable people shy at the soap-box orator and overlook Bertrand Russell in his study. To be considered dangerous, a dramatist must have about him something of the conventionalized radical. Few things are seen until they have become myths. The public that neither reads Shaw nor understands him has a vague mental image of a flaming beard, a sardonic smile, a Jaeger shirt, and a Fenian meeting. That is the real thing; it would make the very Lusk Committee take notice. But John Galsworthy? There are his well-bred early novels; there is his friendship with Winthrop Ames. He has lectured before the Drama League here in a faultless frock-coat. When he was not lecturing he was reserved to the point of taciturnity. How admirable and how British! Promptly the crowd identifies him with another myth, the gentleman, and trusts and approves him.

If in the privacy of his study he is capable of contemptuous irony (one rather doubts it), his temptation

---

[1] *Plays. Fourth Series.* By John Galsworthy.

toward it must be strong. The correctness of his demeanor has endeared him to broad and wealthy bosoms. And all the while, in the laboratory of his mind, with instruments of deadly delicacy and serene precision, he has tested the political and moral pretensions of mankind and found them a blunder and a shame. He has seen legal justice to be a cruel farce, romantic love a delusion, rigid marriage an instrument of stupid torture, the crowd's charity an insult, and its windy opinions the weapons of murder and disgrace. But he has neither cried nor striven and rarely condescended to argue. He has used a pair of balances—exquisite, fragile-looking things under a crystal globe—and weighed the issues of life. And the result of his weighing is more devastating than the rioting of an army with scarlet flags.

Yet he has never forgotten that he is an artist. He has never, to use his own words, set down directly "those theories in which he himself believes," but has let "the phenomena of life and character" tell their own story and point their own moral. He has not always been able to adhere perfectly to the logic and to the rhythm of life. In *The Fugitive,* fine and right as the details are, there are also artifice and, at the end, a touch of violence. But by virtue of the inner control and patience of his mind he has been able to follow the rhythm of life oftener than any other English dramatist, and he has been able to reproduce it more richly

by virtue of his supreme sensitiveness to the true quality of human speech. The wit and eloquence of Shaw
spring from a different impulse and make for a different goal. Galsworthy's dialogue escapes the caging of
the printed page at once. No theatre can contort it, no
actor vulgarize it with the false graces of his trade.
For it is thus that men speak in the eagerness of affairs
or under the sting of passion.

Of the new plays the first, *A Bit of Love,* is undeni-
ably the weakest. The dramaturgic method uses details both of speech and of character which, sound as
they are in themselves, scatter the impression and dilute
the concentration of the central action. That action
has power in itself, but its conclusion is lame. He who
follows Christ is crucified. The curate Strangway refuses either to hold or persecute his wife, who has gone
to the man she always really loved. The people of the
parish rise up against Strangway as a coward and a
pagan. They despise a man who will not fight for what
is his own. The vicar's wife has the kindest intentions.
But she, too, cannot help reminding him that the
Church "is based on a rightful condemnation of wrong-
doing." Strangway leaves, praying for strength "to
love every living thing." Now it is a well-nigh universal experience that the passions of men will not let
them renounce force until they see its pitiful futility.
The curate shows no sense of the plain fact that perse-
cuting his wife would neither have brought her back

nor healed his wounds, and that dragging her back would only have turned her remorse and compassion into active hate. He renounces with vague emotional gestures. These are to be approved; they are not likely to be imitated. He is, in brief, more saint than man. The representation of him as a miniature St. Francis weakens the human validity of the play.

The Foundations is a dramatic picture of the social turmoil of post-war England. Its mood is one of rather desperate gaiety. Things are going to pieces, but it is better to understand and tolerate than to be glum and important. From a little group of consummately drawn characters there stand out Lord William Dromondy, son of a duke and M. P., and Lemmy, gasfitter and uncompromising revolutionist. The bad joke is that these two—quite unlike Anthony and Roberts in *Strife*—are not opposed to each other at all. Lord William knows perfectly well that the game is up. He has been through the war and sees that Lemmy's diagnosis and accusation are alike unanswerable. The capitalist state asked labor to defend it and then "soon as ever there was no dynger from outside, stawted to myke it inside wiv an iron 'and." Lord William quite agrees. But he is in a minority among his own class and no rational course of action seems open to him at all. He holds a meeting to relieve the conditions of sweated labor, but he is aware of the fact that such feeble and gentlemanly tinkering no longer counts. The representative of the press sputters the old phrases for the wage paid him by a capitalist paper, but in his heart he echoes the final cry of the indomitable Lemmy: "Dahn wiv the country, dahn wiv everyfing! Begin agyne from the foundytions!" It is the foundations that must be rebuilt.

The Skin-Game has a more timeless touch. It takes the tragi-comedy of all human conflict, localizes it narrowly, embodies it with the utmost concreteness, and yet exhausts its whole significance. For the staggering truth concerning all human conflict, whether between groups of men or individuals, is that each contestant is both right and wrong; that each has the subjective conviction of being wholly right; that as the conflict grows in length and bitterness each is guilty of deeds that blur his original rightness and bring him closer to the wrongness against which he fights; that hence to be victorious in any conflict is to add your adversary's unrighteousness to your own and to be defeated is to gain the only chance of saving your soul. "Who touches pitch shall be defiled" is the motto of *The Skin-Game*. The pitch that defiled the Hillcrists and the Hornblowers was not in either of them but in the conflict that arose between them. Galsworthy has never derived a dramatic action from deeper sources in the nature of man; he has never put forth a more far-reaching idea nor shown it more adequately in terms of flesh and blood—the gentle Hillcrist who has an intermittent vision of the truth, the too sturdy Hornblower who has none, the clear-eyed, arrowy Jill, the confused and passionate victim Chloe. There are far greater plays in the modern drama—greater in emotional power and imaginative splendor. There is none that illustrates more exactly or searchingly the inner nature, stripped of the accretions of myth and tradition, of the tragic process itself.

Barrie, or The Silver Lining

CONTEMPORARY reviewers of the drama may be divided into three classes: those who debate whether Pinero or Barrie is the greater playwright; those who are troubled over the relative eminence of Barrie and Shaw; those to whom both controversies are barren of content, as hardly related to serious dramatic criticism at all. What relation, let us see, has Barrie to serious drama?

It will be useful to examine the fable of *Mary Rose,* a characteristic play. The Morelands take their little daughter, Mary Rose, on a trip to the outer Hebrides. Left for an hour on a tiny island that has an eerie reputation among the Scotch country-folk, Mary Rose disappears. At the end of thirty days she is found sketching in the very spot whence she had vanished. There is no gap in her consciousness; she thinks she was left a moment before. At times thereafter her mind seems to reach out after a lost memory; but since her parents have told her nothing, her development is normal. At nineteen she is betrothed to a young midshipman to whom the Morelands feel it their duty to communicate the strange adventure of Mary Rose's childhood. Her marriage with Simon Blake is very happy, and when her little son is four years old she persuades

her husband to take her on a fishing trip to the Heb-
ridean islands, of which her memories are quite un-
clouded. On the same fatal islet of her first adventure
she disappears again. This time the years drag on.
Her wild young son runs away to sea at the age of
twelve. Her husband becomes a distinguished naval
officer, but does not marry again. When twenty-five
years have passed and Simon Blake is visiting the
Morelands, a Scotch clergyman who was once the
Blakes's guide comes in and announces that Mary Rose
has reappeared just as she did on that earlier occasion.
She enters, young and fresh as on the far day of her
doom, and finds her parents old and weary and her
husband strange and gray. She asks for her little son
and asks for him in vain. At this point the action of
the play itself ends. The epilogue permits us darkly to
infer that she died of the shock of an estranged world
and her child's absence. For in that epilogue the son,
now a grizzled Australian veteran of the world war,
holds converse in the deserted Moreland house with
her unquiet ghost, which vaguely intimates that on the
island magical music lured her to an abode of blessed
spirits to which she is now fain to return.

It is clear that Barrie did not mean this fable to be
accepted literally, and equally clear that he was not
merely dramatizing a bit of folk-lore. We must look
for the idea about which the action crystallized. We
find it, if anywhere, at the opening of the third act,

immediately prior to the last appearance of Mary Rose.
The Morelands, except for tremulous hands and white
hair, are exactly as they were a quarter of a century
ago.   They question each other and find that the great
and strange tragedy of their lives has left them essentially untouched.   After a little, happiness had come
"breaking through."   Their daughter's unheard-of fate,
the loss of their grandson—these things are now as
though they had hardly been at all.   Time heals.   That
is not a very notable idea, but in a literal sense it is true
enough.   Ideas, however, have their own spiritual qualities, and the fact that time undoubtedly heals may
be regarded in different ways.   There is Shelley's way
of regarding it:

> Alas! that all we love of him should be,
> But for our grief, as if it had not been,
> And grief itself be mortal!

There is the bitterest sting, the long, immedicable woe.
Forgetfulness is the last affront we offer the sacred, un-
resisting dead.   Barrie does not think so.   His famous
whimsical kindliness comes in.   Moreland declares that
he has spent his life pleasantly with pleasant little
things; he is not equal to tragedy; he doesn't know
what to do with it.   The return of Mary Rose makes
him horribly uncomfortable.   He wants to get back
to his collection of prints.   And Barrie sheds the tough,
pink glow of his optimism on this lost soul.   He would

undoubtedly avert his virtuous face from all human
errors due to passion, to excess, to the generous vitality
of nature. His plays are commended for their purity.
He surrounds with his gentlest pathos and all the beauty
he can command a triviality of soul that is as shameful
as one hopes it rare. Spiritual triviality—we come very
close to Barrie with that phrase. He makes harsh
things sweetish and grave things frivolous and noble
things to seem of small account. No wonder he is
popular among all the shedders of easy, comfortable
tears. He dramatizes the cloud in order to display its
silver lining.

Mary Rose is as incoherent in its imaginative structure as it is false and feeble in idea. If the mysterious
world to which the island gives access is an abode of
the dead, why is the living Mary Rose permitted twice
to enter? If it is not, why does the same music summon the wandering ghost that once lured the living
girl? Why does she leave the blessed islands of the
dead to haunt the decaying house? Do those islands
give neither forgetfulness nor knowledge? Why does
a distinguished naval officer permit his twelve-year-old
son gradually to disappear in Australia? Would not
a cablegram have caused the child to be recovered and
sent home? Must he be lost only to give the ghost of
Mary Rose an excuse for haunting the house? Was
there some special purpose in making him so rough a
customer that he converses with his dead mother in

gutter slang? Did that circumstance add an extra luster to the silver lining? Vain questions. Barrie's imagination is as uncontrolled as his ideas are feeble and conventional. Yet this is the dramatist whose position in permanent literature is seriously debated. This purveyor of sentimental comedy to the unthinking crowd deceives the semi-judicious by moments of literary charm and deftness and mellow grace that recall the years when he wrote *Sentimental Tommie* and *Margaret Ogilvie*. But those years are gone. His noisy stage successes have left him increasingly bare of scruple, of seriousness, of artistic and intellectual coherence. They have left him "whimsical" and false and defeated in the midst of wealth and fame.

Archer, or Loaded Dice

AN audience of extraordinary distinction gathered at
the Booth Theatre one night to witness the first performance of *The Green Goddess* by Mr. William
Archer. Academic powers and principalities displayed
both easy majesty and graceful unbending. The literary and editorial world had sent its emissaries. Some
unsophisticated youth aspiring to the honors of letters
and of learning would have been abashed by such a
blaze of glory. To one who was neither young nor
unsophisticated the splendor of the scene was not untouched by gloom. Mr. Winthrop Ames, it is true,
lived up to the fondest expectations of his cultured
friends. The scenic production was superb in shape
and color and rich verisimilitude. There were group
scenes—barbaric warriors with dark shields and slant-
ing spears silhouetted against a burning sky—that took
one's breath away; there was a room in the rajah's
palace where faultless beauty spoke of malignity in
every detail. It is also true that Mr. George Arliss
gave a performance of such pliancy and precision that
he seemed to flash and darken like a polished blade in
alternate sunshine and shadow, that Mr. Ivan Simpson
was of an astonishing raciness and truth, and that Mr.

Cyril Keightly and Miss Olive Wyndham displayed
their considerable talents to the best advantage. Nor
must one forget that, at the appropriate moment, Mr.
Arliss made a curtain speech whose easy elegance was
a triumph of the art which conceals art, and that the
distinguished dramatic critic and translator of Ibsen
followed him in one that added weightiness to grace
and glow to sparkle And yet that touch of gloom persisted.

For all this pomp and circumstance was secondary.
There was, after all, a play. And the fable of that
play is as follows: Two British officers and a woman,
unhappily wed to one, chastely adored by the other,
crash down in their airplane over the remotest Hima-
layas into the unknown principality of Rookh. While
the rajah is being summoned, the three sit in the left
of the stage-picture and explain to each other their
most guarded but common secrets. This is what is
known as exposition. The rajah comes and offers them
a sophisticated European hospitality. He has taken an
honors degree at Cambridge and is, on one side of his
nature, a cynical, dry-souled man of the world. But
his deeper and ancestral self is at one with his tribes-
men of the hills. Three sons of his father have just
been condemned to death in India; his opportunity for
revenge is at hand. Need one take the trouble to add
that the rajah makes improper proposals to the English lady, that her unnecessary husband is shot, not,

however, before he has sent to India a wireless call
for help, or that, at the precise moment when the lady
and the man of her spotless affections are about to be
tortured and sacrificed to the green goddess, the British
planes are heard metallically whirring in the air and
the bombs of warning and liberation drop? Needed one
to add that?   Oak and triple brass must have surrounded Mr. Archer's heart when in the evening of his
days he set out to compete with the early romances of
Rider Haggard. Dramatic critics need not write plays
at all. Nor if they do, need they write good plays.
But can one, to take an apposite example, imagine
Jules Lemaître writing not *Le Pardon* nor *L'Age dif-
ficile* but—*La Femme X——?*

In Mr. Archer's breast, however, as in Faust's, two
souls have always dwelled. He has done magnificent
service in introducing Ibsen to the English-speaking
public. He has also written a book called *Play-making*
which is widely used as a text-book and contains a chap-
ter called *Chance and Coincidence*. Here he wrote:
"The stage is the realm of appearances, not of realities,
where paste jewels are at least as effective as real ones."
If this referred to a ballerina's necklace it would be
true. But it refers to much more and so becomes dan-
gerously untrue. The world itself is only a world of
appearances. The drama seeks to interpret the spiritual meaning of that phenomenal order by an act of
heightened and condensed and clarified imitation. It

must be, in a sense, more real, more packed with reality than any fragment of the sprawling, shifting world of appearances; it holds fast a concentrated bit of reality for our contemplation. It does that or it is nothing. And further Mr. Archer wrote: "The playwright is perfectly justified in letting chance play its probable and even inevitable part in the affairs of his characters." That is very loose and very inaccurate thinking. For what is a chance or an accident? It is the event of a chain of causality that our vision does not embrace. Could we grasp the universe entire and be privy to all its workings, chance and accident would disappear. They are brief names for a necessary ignorance. But it is the aim of the dramatist to make life more and not less intelligible. It is his first business, so far as it is humanly speaking possible, to command all the chains of causality that explain the events with which he deals. The wise Greeks derived chance from the inexorable will of a fate to which even the gods were subject. They made it part of their universal order. Mr. Archer really means sudden intrusion of the uncaused. But the uncaused does not exist. The serious modern dramatist who admits accident or chance is not unlike a chemist who should assist recalcitrant nature to produce the specious show of a successful result to an experiment by the injection of substances that negate the experiment's entire purpose and meaning. The artist, to be sure, is fallible. He works with treacherous and imponderable materials. His severest masterpiece will seem to him still not inevitable enough. He must be content if, in his innermost consciousness, he knows that it has grown and has not been made. Mr. Archer protests that, in spite of his statements, he does not like to see the dice loaded. To admit chance, accident, or inexplicable coincidence at all is to load the dramatic dice at the very outset. Once you do that you can translate Ibsen and write *The Green Goddess* with equal cheerfulness. But the grim old Norseman among the shades would understand the touch of gloom that would not, to two or three people, lift from the Booth Theatre on a certain night.

Somerset Maugham Himself

FOR several centuries the drama has been the outcast of English literature. Men thought it good enough as a source of fortune but hardly as a source of fame. Its supposed technique kept them from using it as a vehicle of true expression; a mingled contempt and reverence for their audiences held in check their impulses toward veracity and power. The man who wrote *Tom Jones* threw off nearly a score of now forgotten comedies; the man who wrote *Of Human Bondage* is responsible for as many. But Fielding's action was the more natural. There was not in any vital sense an expressive drama in the England of his day. Nor could he have borrowed fruitfully from the tragedy of Voltaire or the comedy of Marivaux. Mr. Maugham has had the example of Shaw and of Galsworthy and of the Germans among whom he passed his student years. Yet he has gone so far, in the past, as to write for the stage with a hard deliberateness from within the round of illusions he must himself despise. He sank as low as *Cæsar's Wife*. Perhaps a late uneasiness assailed him. He heeded that warning and wrote *The Circle*.

He does not yet venture a tone that fits his subject and his fundamental mood. He lets the irony lighten

and brighten and become farcical; he lingers and hesitates until one almost believes that he is at one with
the trivial Pinero who thought that Paula Tanqueray
was really an object of tragic compassion because the
ladies of the county would not come to tea. Late in the
third act the cleaving truth appears. But even here
Mr. Maugham will not let it be quite somber or else
quite radiant. He swathes it a little with sentiment
and muffles it a little with false memories. But it is
out. For the first time in the drama his intellectual
integrity is intact.

Two subjects seem to haunt the mind of the British
playwright: the subject of the socially unequal marriage and the subject of the eloping couple who drag
out hopeless lives because their particular social group
will have none of them. And the tradition was that
the first of these two actions should end happily, as in
Robertson's *Caste,* and that the second should end
wretchedly and vindicate the social solidarity of the
British ruling class. Galsworthy's *The Eldest Son*
shattered the first of these traditional solutions, Somerset Maugham's *The Circle* shatters the second.

At first the conventional tone seems to prevail. Lord
Porteous and Lady Kitty who ran away together thirty
years ago return. They quarrel and bicker. He gets
tight after dinner because he had to give up his political career and could not go big game shooting with his
equals. She is rouged and affected, old without peace

or dignity or comfort, because during the thirty years
in Italy she had no place or activity in society and had
to consort with kept women and shady barons. The
once abandoned husband circles about these two with
an old bitterness sheathed in a bright, luxurious, goad-
ing irony. But the mere visible example of Porteous
and Lady Kitty does not suffice to point the moral of
their fate. Elizabeth, Lady Kitty's slim and fiery and
romantic young daughter-in-law, is just about to bolt
with a young man from the Malay Peninsula. Porteous and Lady Kitty do a brave and ghastly thing.
They bare their history. Its boredom, its moral seedi-
ness, its brief rapture, and its long regret. Elizabeth
is frightened and subdued. But her young man makes
a final plea. He does not offer her happiness but splendor and despair, not the peace of the world but the
sword of the spirit. She goes with him. And as she
goes old Porteous rises to a moment of self-recognition
that saves the play, crushes a sentimental convention
of the stage, and vindicates the mind and art of Somerset Maugham. He and Lady Kitty have failed not
on account of what they did but on account of what
they were. "We're trivial people, Kitty," he says sadly.
It is the right and momentous word, the word that
Pinero did not utter even by implication in regard to
the Tanquerays. People who go to pieces morally and
mentally simply because the members of one small social group cast them off and who therefore herd with

pinchbeck imitations of that group are trivial people. The world is wide and full of magnificent persons from all its ends who do not ask after the social register. They whom the social register can bend were never erect in any deeply human sense. It is character that creates the quality of action. Not what you do matters, but what your soul makes of the thing you do.

It will be seen, then, that with *The Circle* Somerset Maugham at last approaches the serious modern drama —the drama in which conflict and solution are transferred from the superficial compacts and modes of social life into that realm of the reason and of spiritual values in which those modes and compacts are themselves questionable and on trial. This is indeed the test of any play: whether it accepts the rules of the social or political or moral game as fixed and final or whether it goes to those sources of truth in the nature of man and of his world which these rules often slander and betray. The hardest thing to do, Maugham wrote in his great novel, is to "establish a contact with reality." It seems hardest of all through the medium of the drama. But in *The Circle* he has established that contact at last.

Max Reinhardt

IT is not often that a man retiring from public activity at the age of forty-eight may be said to have changed permanently the character of the art which he has practised. Yet to say that of Max Reinhardt is, in one sense, to say too little. It may be justly urged, from another point of view, that he has created a new art or, at the least, transformed a professional activity into a creative one. For the essence of this man's work is not to be sought in his revolving stages, his tiny or gigantic playhouses, or even in the unexampled wealth of great dramatic literature which he persuaded his public to accept. His secret is his inner and initial conception of his task; his triumph is in the lonely hours of contemplation before his vision was transferred to the theatre.

What was the character of the vision that came to him? It was a vision of the play's soul, of its innermost nature in terms of images and sounds. What came to him was the play's intimate "style," its inner music, its inevitable rhythm of tone and color. The sudden vision revealed to him how, in this special instance, the "intensity of nature" could be equaled—the intensity of the play's own interpretation of nature, be it observed. For Reinhardt's imagination is synthetic, not analytic. He spent his apprenticeship with Otto Brahm, first of the great naturalistic directors. But he himself is a neo-romantic through and through. Hence his close affiliation with Hofmannsthal and the younger members of the Viennese school; hence in so many of his stage-pictures the eerie grace and wild, haunting loveliness that allies him to the spirit of Moritz von Schwind and the romantic painters. The vision that came to him was, in brief, one of a special kind of beauty answering a special soul in art. So, brooding over *A Midsummer Night's Dream*, it came to him that this piece was a forest poem—Waldgedicht. He saw the forest in its changing moods; he saw the creatures of the play blend with or detach themselves from the trees and glades. He heard the forest music. He saw and created a vision of the forest—Shakespeare's and also his own. The spectators were persuaded to yield imaginatively to the vision and this now celebrated production was performed nearly a thousand times! What the "sacred bard" is to the hero, Reinhardt has been to the bard himself.

Having seen his vision, he forced himself to work with all the national passion for scholarly thoroughness and accuracy. He read the commentators of the poet and the play, the political history of the play's period, the history of its manners and its art. But his intention was never realistic reproduction, never a cold historicity; he sought the symbolical detail that blended with and interpreted his original vision. Thus in working at his production of *Othello* he found that the rhythm of color which his imaginative grasp of the Venice of 1500 had awakened in him was almost exactly identical with that employed by Carpaccio. And so the whole play was embodied through a restricted scale of tints: leaf-green, yellowish white, gray, brown, brick-red. But in the scenes at Cyprus line and color, within the framework of his own vision and Carpaccio's testimony, were given an added sweep and a touch of sultriness. For here, in spite of the Venetian domination, the Orient began to glow and throb.

Such details and a thousand others Reinhardt recorded in a document known as his Regiebuch. It contained the text of the play and a paraphrase of that text giving the most exhaustive directions for the physical embodiment of his vision. Not until this document was completed did he call his assistants into conference; not until his creative work was done did he enter his workshops or his theatres. And often, after many weeks of labor, he would reject an entire production at its final rehearsal. The vision had been lost; the rhythm was somehow broken; the special beauty he had dreamed had not been born. In that spirit and in no other does art come into being. The perfect and permanent things are difficult and rare. No wonder that it took this man less than twenty years to revolutionize the theatre of his country.

His concrete creation of the beauty through which he sought to equal the intensity of nature in terms of mood and light and line and color may be studied in some of his stage-pictures. Take the scene of the banquet in *Macbeth*. Every line is a straight line, every angle a right angle. All form is reduced to a barbaric severity. But the two rectangular windows in the background through which the cold Northern stars glitter are narrow and tall—so unimaginably tall that they seem to touch that sky of doom. The torches turn the rough brown of the primitive wooden walls to a tarnished bronze. Only on the rude tables lie splashes of menacing yellow. There is something barren and gigantic about the scene—a sinister quiet, a dull presage. Contrast with this the desolate modernity, the spiritual malady expressed in the upper chamber in *John Gabriel Borkman,* or the splendor and gay yet pain-touched passion in *Much Ado About Nothing,* or the earnest charm and cool, autumnal grace of *The Marriage of Figaro.* These scenes have body. But that body is irradiated by a spiritual life. And that life expresses the creative vision of Max Reinhardt.

IV
Art, Life and the Theatre

A Certain Playwright

EMERGING from the lower East Side, he made his first appearance on the campus of a well-known university. The emaciated little figure in rough, baggy clothes seemed even then but a passing accident that would soon yield to the natural breadth and sturdiness befitting a mind so vigorous and resolute. In a flat almost unmodeled face one saw, first and last, the small, dark, indomitable eyes that could melt into kindliness or harden into a militant shrewdness. There was not a shred of affection about him and the lock of hair that slanted across his forehead marked him as an intellectual. He meant to write plays—plays that would get on. He had already contacts of some sort with casual purveyors of vaudeville material and he let you know with a grim and almost contemptuous good humor that your pleasant idealisms would get you exactly nowhere. He studied the great dramatists of several literatures. He had both the mind and the humanity to understand their virtues. But these, he informed you, were remote and impossible. A teacher of deep personal strength, drenched in the stream of reality, unattenuated by academic repression and refinement, might have stirred him. He met none such and listened with mild approval to the blithe, learned, and immensely accomplished gentleman whose notions, despite a flourishing of great names and works, were at bottom identical with his own. It is at this point that his story begins to broaden in meaning. The university taught him many things, but it produced in him no inner change. It had, in no deep sense, held him, and he turned—you could almost see the doggedness of his attack—to crash through the obstacles that arose between himself and Broadway. He disappeared from view into a half-murky, half-garish world of vaudeville sketches and of small collaborations with tinseled semi-celebrities of the stage. According to his own notion he was mastering his chosen craft.

He mastered it. He crushed the obstacles. But it took him fourteen years. Of those years no direct knowledge is available. But our friend's deliberately direct gestures both of mind and body had never quite concealed a lurking sensitiveness of the spirit. Perhaps he attempted to write more truly and nobly than his theories warranted, and indeed got nowhere; perhaps such experiences caused him to harden both his temper and his methods the more rigorously. One can easily divine moments of half-success and moments of empty despair. Both were but spurs to his tireless energy. Suddenly, from any public point of view—at last, of course, from his own—he burst with quite unparalleled resoundingness upon the living stage. At

the end of a single season he had three popular successes of the first order to his credit. The houses were
thronged, road companies started West and South; a
golden flood poured in on him. He was to be seen
everywhere. Managers, actors, fellow playwrights
treated him with a caressing familiarity. You could
see him in a box at first nights, now broad and stocky
and more than ever full of strength and tenacity. But
the flat face was lined and almost scarred here and
there, and the clever, kindly eyes passed from satisfaction to melancholy. For, strange to say, the critics
held out against him, and he, a man of scholarly training and hidden sensitiveness, shivered amid the heat
of his success. He wanted them on his side. Were
they not always ready to praise work upon no higher
plane than his own? He was, to be sure, writing down
to the taste of the largest and least discriminating public. But so was everybody else. Only he did it more
effectively, with a hard, merciless, almost brutal knowledge of human weakness and fatuity. The public wept
at his first piece, were thrilled by his second, laughed
with him at his third. He had conquered the stage of
his own day and country, as his old teacher had bidden
him to do; he did well what everybody else was trying
to do and usually did ill. But the critics jeered. Perhaps they were irritated by the very assurance of the
steely cleverness with which, especially in his third
piece, he played upon the showy hypocrisy and hidden

wantonness of his wretched audiences; perhaps they
rebelled against the too terribly calculated succession
of falsely tense moments in his second. The fact remains. And, as that first magnificent season of his
progressed, he grew somber over the situation in which
he found himself—successful by all the avowed standards of his profession and yet denied any ultimate rec-
ognition besides his profits—and once, at least, broke
out in irritation and anger.

How deeply he felt that situation soon became clear.
The first play of his second season told his own story
and symbolized his own defense. A group of college
seniors meet on graduation night and discuss their future. Their confidence in themselves and in each other
is boundless. By common consent one among them,
the poet and idealist, is doomed always to fail and to
depend upon his friends for his worldly welfare. At
the end of three years they meet and, as it is easy to
suspect, the soaring hopes have all gone under and the
friends have only humiliating confessions to make. At
the last moment the poet comes in. He alone has conquered the world; he alone is rich. He has not written
poetry, to be sure. He is, indeed, a garbage king. But
he alone, to whom material things meant least, has
beaten the world at its own vile game. He, too, it becomes clear as the play goes on, has not only conquered
circumstances, but, secure in the riches of his own
mind, has the magnanimity to cast the wealth aside.

The play failed. No critic saw the personal meaning or the pathos of the fable. None suspected an apologue. Nor were the critics to be blamed. For the idea of the play had no embodiment that was worthy of it. Our friend had learned no new methods in a single summer by which to project dramatically the realities of his own soul. Characters, incident, mechanism were of the old insufferable hollowness and artifice. Only the cold dexterity, the unscrupulous theatrical skill—these were lacking. The man, laying bare his heart, had ruined the playwright.

On the second night of the play's brief run he stood in the vestibule of the theatre, gesticulating with his short, thick arms. The reviews that morning had been contemptuous to the point of ferocity. "Did you see the papers?" he cried. "What's the use of writing honestly, of giving them good stuff? What's the use?" The ushers were putting out the lights in the theatre, the audience had melted away, even the vestibule grew dim. He continued to stand in the shadow, expostulating with vigor, with characteristic tenacity, yet with a strange and almost boyish helplessness of appeal. What was one to tell him? That his whole art must be born again? That he must forget all he had slowly learned, all his own resolves? That he must return to early memories or purely human impressions and write as simply as though he had never known a theatre? That collaboration, despite misleading examples in another age, is the death of true art, which must arise, like prayer, from the lonely chambers of the soul? That his powerful intelligence, his generous gifts, his wide knowledge would avail him nothing without a shifting of his whole vision of man and life and art? He turned at last to go, thrusting his broad shoulders forward with a movement half of disgust, half of determination. His whole body, in its vigorous expressiveness, seemed to say that never had the futile absurdity of his inmost self with its sounder impulses become more clear. He walked up the dark alley beside the theatre on his way to the players' rooms and disappeared. He will pass, in all likelihood, from one loud success to another and, amid the plaudits of the crowd and the wealth of the years, hide ever more guardedly the undying ache in his own soul.

Within Our Gates

LET US suppose that, among the many thousands of visitors who throng New York during the fall and winter months, there were also to be found one of those forlorn children of light whom Matthew Arnold was fond of mentioning. It might even be some college professor from the West or the Middle West. Such things have been known. He has probably taught through a long winter and also, in order to save a little money, through a dusty summer. He has lectured on the drama, its development and technique, but has seen nothing for many, many months except Mary Pickford on the screen and once Mr. Robert Mantell as Macbeth. And now the air of Broadway tingles on his face and his great moment has come. He is here to draw inner sustenance for another two or three years. And luckily—oh, yes, such things happen too—he has moneyed friends here to whom theatre tickets (war-tax and all) are unconsidered trifles. His host is down-town on business. But his hostess is admirably present and sympathetic. Of course, he must see the new plays! She quietly observes him, poor dear, with his blending of a becoming gravity and a boyish eagerness. She decides against box-seats and first nights. He hasn't

probably—again, poor dear!—the proper clothes. She
scans the paper. The sunlight falls on the permanent
Marcelle waves of her hair. The Professor, once her
classmate, decides that the art and air of the metropolis make for youth. She must be quite . . . The
hostess interrupts his reflections. "Marjorie Rambeau
is at the Maxine Elliott in a new play. How lucky!
She's perfectly wonderful. And they say that *Wedding Bells* at the Harris is quite adorable. Such a
good cast, too. And of course you're not to miss *The
Son-Daughter,* Mr. Belasco's new production. Most
artistic, you may be sure. You'll love it!" Already a
little shadow creeps into the Professor's mind. She
mentions no authors. By whom are these plays? But
he is shy, and his two glittering weeks are all before
him, and he determines to let her be his guide.

He couldn't, somehow, share his friend's exuberant
enthusiasm for Miss Rambeau. He admitted that the
play, *The Unknown Woman,* put together by three
people of whom he had never heard, was preposterous.
He told his hostess that it was kept going only through
a voluntary suspension of common sense on the part
of both characters and audience. Nevertheless, he
could not help feeling that Miss Rambeau's intensity
need not have had that edge of roughness. There was
a twang in it, as of a brazen string. He honestly
thought the part of the fat ward-heeler the best taken
in the play, and his hostess concluded that learned peo-

ple have their own crudities. The surface of her brilliant eagerness to amuse him was slightly dimmed.

The Professor did enjoy *Wedding Bells*. Again, although he thought he knew the history of the recent drama moderately well, the name of the author had no associations for him. And again the fable of the play was silly beyond belief. But he yielded himself gladly to the verve and sprightliness and obvious intelligence of the acting. It was not hidden from him that Wallace Eddinger's mannerisms were merely stereotyped mannerisms carried from play to play. But to him they were not stale. And he was delighted by Miss Margaret Lawrence's suave brightness and intellectual grace and by the full, rich flavor—like that of good ale—of John Harwood's performance. His hostess was perceptibly cheered, and at once ordered magnificent seats for the next night at the Belasco Theatre. She anticipated a wonderful moment.

The solemn splendor of the playhouse's interior attuned the innocent Professor to a mood of lofty expectation. He was thrilled by the lovely sound of the bell that signaled the rising of the curtain. But he gazed and listened with a growing astonishment and finally with a sardonic smile. Tucked in his hostess's car he spoke, poor man, with that touch of the didactic which polite people deplore in his kind, and with a virility of diction that would come out whenever he was at a safe distance from his dean and his president:

"To smother such inhuman and debased drivel in Chinese objects of art that are worth a fortune is the last insult to the art of the theatre and the public intelligence. It's literally trying to make a silk purse out of a ——" His hostess interrupted him with infinite delicacy and skill and made a mental reckoning of the number of days her friend had still to be entertained.

But she was really as heroic as she was kind. She made appropriate inquiries and took the Professor to the haunts of a supposedly more authentic art. He followed her gladly, though now with an inner wariness. He saw Lennox Robinson's *The Lost Leader* at the Greenwich Village Theatre, and sorrowfully recognized a noble intention unsupported by either dramatic or intellectual power, so that the play trailed off into a babble of empty verbiage. He wondered how so clever a man as Frank Conroy could have been taken in by so sterile and ineffectual a play. He was frankly amused by the amateurs who spouted the sociological platitudes of yesteryear at the delightfully built little Bramhall Playhouse. Nor was he unaware of the pathos of the discrepancy between its manager's aspirations and abilities. He went to MacDougal Street and saw the Provincetown Players (of whose former seasons he had heard good reports) indulge in banalities no less annoying for their frenzied queerness, and found confirmation of his old adage that freedom in the life of art and of the intellect is unattainable by febrile temperaments without either knowledge or power. He went to the opening bill of the Théâtre Parisien at the Belmont Theatre and saw a hard, chill, shallow little comedy of amorous intrigue performed with unmistakable skill, but in an almost archaic tradition of the art of acting. He also heard there a little opera bouffe charmingly sung. And he enjoyed one melody by Claude Terrasse so much that, with his incurable touch of rusticity, he hummed it on the way to his hostess's house.

That lady felt both righteous and relieved on the day of her friend's departure. She was far too busy to reflect, but he gave her an uneasy sense of his intellectual remoteness. She was too clever not to have been able to follow the paths of his thinking, but she was far too comfortable in her present mental condition to attempt it. The Professor, vastly stimulated by his experiences despite his obvious disappointments, mulled over on his westward-speeding train the outline of a lecture which his local Drama League Center would find immensely acceptable later in the winter. Certain sentences formed themselves in his mind with a rare inevitableness and ease: "Great wealth is being expended on our American theatre, and there is no dearth of admirable talent among our actors and our craftsmen of the stage. But all this wealth and talent are left wholly sterile through the lack of a directing intelligence. The managers are commercial opportunists who have not yet attained the ordinary business man's instinct to employ experts. They are advised by 'cheap' people to do 'cheap' things that are supposed to be unfailingly successful and are, in fact, the wildest gambles. Good plays, selected by sound judges, would probably average quite as high a number of commercial successes as the pieces now produced. Hence the central problem is assuredly this: to make the managerial mind more accessible to the influence of the best available knowledge and judgment in its own field. . . ." Whether, for one wild and half-waggish moment, the Professor had a vision of himself lifted out of his poverty and appointed dramaturgic director of some metropolitan manager at a fabulous salary, history does not record.

Play-Making

AT a Broadway opening one night the play-bill instructed the audience that the new drama to be presented was "by Margaret Lane and Howard Jack." These names at least serve to veil the crude facts, preserve the moral, and guard the proprieties. Below was the further information, subdued by smaller type and a pair of parentheses, that the work of these authors was "based on a play by Milton Davis." It was no masterpiece. It has already gone the way of many of these noisy concoctions. But a clever actress played the chief part, and the first night audience glowed and applauded, and there was a flutter of enthusiastic visiting in the stalls and boxes. Indiscriminate and slightly illiterate adjectives hummed in the air. At the appropriate moment there was a loud and persistent call for the author. Needless to say that these play-makers and press agents, costumers and actresses out of work, friends, "fans," and scene painters had no desire to rouse Mr. Milton Davis, who was, after all, the "onlie begetter" of the evening's masterpiece, out of his decent obscurity. Nor was their applause more than perfunctory when Miss Margaret Lane, a stout, scared lady, blinked for a forlorn moment across the footlights. It was the great Mr. Howard Jack whom the audience desired to see. He came—large, lustrous, easy, commanding. He leaned on a polished cane and his top-hat flashed. Diamonds twinkled from his studs and waistcoat buttons. A large-boned, pink, crudely impressive man, radiating success, monarch of the scene he surveyed. He made the desired curtain speech. He explained, not without wit and adroitness, that more and more as time went on he had to neglect his own work and act the part of a "play surgeon." Managers had promising "scripts"—as had been the case here—but the plays were not in shape to please the public. Then he was called in to cut, re-write, and stage. It was a humble office but a necessary one. At last he had found a name for it. A tumult of respect and affection followed him into the wings. In how many bosoms glowed the hope that some day a shy little manuscript now hidden in some managerial safe would attract the lordly eye of Mr. Jack and become a roaring Broadway hit! How many brown and blond and black little heads thought of the many plays full of the "cutest" parts which it was the great man's privilege to cast! Why should they not applaud him? It was a touching scene.

Mr. Howard Jack is not the only unerring judge of the public heart. There are others who infuse "pep," "punch," and patriotism into the plays on which they operate. And sometimes these processes have a history which is not nearly so gay as the result. We do not know, for that matter, the feelings of the shadowy

Milton Davis. We happen to know, on the other hand, the inner and most instructive history of another case. About five years ago a young playwright, lacking neither talent, mind, nor character, hit upon an ingenious technical device and a popular fable. His play was very successful. The managers asked for more. But our friend had other notions concerning his art. A melodrama was well enough. You made a little money with it in order to devote yourself to your true business. He wrote, to use his own words, "fantasy, naked tragedy, satiric comedy, psychological drama." The managers would have none of it. They demanded another *Day in Court*. One cannot live on the royalties of a single play forever. The young playwright wrote another ingenious melodrama. But he saw no reason why even into such a play one might not weave a little truth, some threads of intellectual honesty. In the center of his action he therefore placed an artist who, in a lurid enough way, does symbolize an eternal human conflict. The rest was stage carpentry. But our playwright had sacrificed briefly to his true gods. A great authority, a greater than Mr. Jack—the pundit of pundits—refused the play. The artist, he said curtly, "would get a laugh." A somewhat less magnificent personage condescended to explain. "No artist is ever taken seriously by an audience." Hence the man in the stalls "has no interest in seeing him killed." And since the melodrama is a mimic man-hunt, to arouse such an interest is to win one's battle. At this point the play surgeons entered the game. Their task was to dehumanize the author's protagonist and to reduce the whole play to a consistently melodramatic level. One suggested turning the artist into a licentious club man. The author refused. A lady surgeon, herself a writer who ought to be above such things, advised making him a psychoanalyst. Then the "star" took a hand. He had been selected to play, not, of course, the now plainly wicked artist-clubman-doctor, but the righteous district attorney who brings the rogue to justice and marries the heroine. This gentleman declared that the doctor was still "far too human." He might "steal the play from the star!" Preliminary performances, held on the road, turned the poor artist of the original play not only into a knave, but into a "nigger." The star, furthermore, interpolated for himself a number of burly and sentimental and patriotic lines which he copyrighted in his own name. To the dismayed author hurrying across the continent to save some rag of his artistic decency, a flat ultimatum was presented. The play is a success. The villain is killed every night to the glee of the stalls. The author's name shimmers in electric lights. He is making money; he is envied. His real work lies in his desk. The play surgeons will continue to share his earnings. For he will try again to write not quite as badly as one can. But he must live.

There are tailor-made plays. A popular star cannot find a medium for his art. That statement which one hears so often is, if literally accepted, sheer nonsense. What the star means is that there exists, naturally enough, no play in the world in which he can exploit his personal mannerisms and favorite tricks in the center of the stage throughout an evening. The masters, alas, did not foresee him. In reality he does not want to act, but, like Tom Sawyer, to show off. Hence he himself or his sister or his wife writes a dramatic entertainment about him in his most successful and fetching poses. But the manuscript has not yet the requisite theatrical "pep" and "punch." Enter the play surgeon as co-author.

There are ghost plays. A young author has a manuscript. One of the great play surgeons sees possibilities in it. A contract is drawn up according to which the surgeon has the right to make any and all changes he sees fit. The surgeon also figures as chief author and receives, contractually, two-thirds of all royalties. The young author, who is something of an artist, is ashamed of his bargain. But he must live. Such is the art of play-making, the noble comradeship of collaboration! Learned professors speak of collaboration and think of Beaumont and Fletcher. They should remember the elder Dumas and his methods of manufacturing literature. His example lives and thrives.

Conversation

THE dark and distinguished playwright on the sofa was deliberately drifting into confidences. But the art by which he gained his effects had just a touch of crudity. He forced the note too briskly and took for granted the mood he should have striven to create. The critic, watching him from a deep chair, was not surprised. The playwright was good-looking and firmly intelligent. But all his surfaces, from his boots to his cheeks, were too unfurrowed. He had obviously been born in his particular Zion and all his efforts to prove that he was not at ease in it seemed rather pointless. Nor had anyone asked him so suddenly to justify his soul. The room was a trifle chill, the afternoon light far from mellow, the beverage only tea. Other matters, too, on which the men agreed admirably were not lacking. But the playwright had, as the critic observed with a faint twinge of vicarious shame, set himself a definite task. He crossed his legs and leaned back with elaborate casualness:

"What is one to do? You must either remain unperformed or adopt the public's point of view about life."

"Or what it thinks its point of view," the critic said. But he saw at once that his mildness had prevented the

words from reaching his friend's mind. The latter
went on: "And it must be done thoroughly. Half-way
measures are useless. Unless your manager owns his
house he can't keep a play on that plays to less than
eight thousand a week. The rentals are getting pro-
hibitive. Cheaper and noisier things are clamoring to
go on. To get even that chance you must cultivate
people of all sorts, attend to the publicity work—others always bungle it—and spend the greater part of
your time on anything but your job."

The critic, afraid now that he was being cultivated,
stirred his tea. He felt rather dreary. He wanted to
say: "If it's so repulsive, why stick to it? You could
do a dozen other things. One doesn't have to write
plays." But before his small courage to inflict a probably futile sting rose to the point of speech, the other,
now with a pseudo-lyrical intonation, cried: "O for a
hermitage! Of course I do my own, my real work at
intervals. There are my unplayed plays. I'll send you
the new volume that is about to appear."

The cat—a well-bred and not too obtrusive animal—
was out of the bag. But a little flame leaped up, as
it will now and then, in the critic's brain. "I'm sorry,"
he said, "but I can't admit your clearly implicit plea.
I want to believe in what you call your real work, but
I mustn't let you think it possible. You've written
The Adventure of Flip and *Jack and Jill*. You not
only built the false and therefore immoral fables, but

achieved the rancid emotionalism of the dialogue. I don't blame you for trying. Money tempts the best of us. It buys freedom. I blame you for succeeding. Your ability to succeed proves that you are not a native of the regions from which, as you think, the condition of the theatre exiles you. You are at home here —a skilful playwright, and, privately, a cultivated gentleman. But you'll never find your hermitage. Since it was not in your mind from the beginning, it exists on neither sea nor land."

With fantastic suddenness the conversation became general and amid the hubbub and tinkle the blond and energetic playwright came in. His voice was resonant but monotonous. It had a little edge that kept rasping some nerve. "Ah, Charlie's play! Have you seen it? Charming. Oh, charming. But there were mistakes in it at first. He sent for me during the rehearsals. 'Frank,' he said, 'what's wrong with it?' I saw at once. The girl came on too soon; no preparation. In the second place, the jokes would never reach the stalls. They weren't led up to nor repeated." With a kindly and instructive gesture he turned to the critic: "The way it's done in vaudeville, you know. Now everything is right and it's playing to nine thousand a week."

The dark playwright leaned forward. "That's bully! Of course it's a smaller house. *Jack and Jill* did nearly fourteen thousand dollars' worth of business last week." He got up and strolled toward a window while the

blond playwright turned to the critic, who felt the
bleakness in his bones that he always does when he
hears brokers talk. He wanted to go home. But those
glossy eyes held him. "Haven't seen you since the first
night of *Millions Don't Make the Man*. That didn't
do so well. I've got a new thing going on that might interest you. But my real work's more in your line.
Highly imaginative. Like Barrie. We're through with
the ugly. I'll send you the volume in advance of publication."

The critic sank deeper into his chair. The blond
playwright was so sure of himself. But just then he
seemed to withdraw to an inner contemplation of his
own assurance, and from farther down the room came
the Voice which the critic specially dreaded. It was
not rivalry or envy, Heaven knows, that made him
dread the other critic. It was the icy moment of terror
that he always feels when unbridgable chasms open
between his mind and another's. But the Voice arose:
"I admit the merits of *The Brothers*. But its success
or failure will not affect the development of a native
school of drama. Tragedy is foreign to us."

The critic jumped from his chair. A lady regarded
his rude suddenness deprecatingly. But he was beyond
the reach of her rebuke. "Then we are less than human," he cried, "or more. The tragic is in art because
it is in life! Why is nine-tenths of all great literature
shot through and through with tragedy? Because hu-

man life is. The very Fool in Shakespeare has a somber heart, the very grotesques of Dickens throw a
shadow on the understanding mind. If tragedy is foreign to us, then so are birth and love and death and all
spiritual conflict, then we are apes or gods but not
men!" The critic gasped. He hadn't meant to preach.
He was known as a sinister "highbrow" even so. He
smiled wryly. "Have it your own way," he said. "But
what a world you're making: bevo instead of beer,
drug-shops instead of taverns, flirting instead of love,
shop-work instead of Greek, business instead of beauty,
and *Tillie's Triumphs* instead of tragedy!"

With cool precision the Voice—it seemed a collective
Voice—floated above the dead silence: "You do not
understand the theatre."

"And you," retorted the critic wearily, "understand
nothing else."

He turned and, by some magic, found his coat and
hat ready to his hand. Outside the bluish dark was
splashed by the lights of Broadway. The stars had no
chance against that glitter. He walked in the oppo-
site direction. He needed a peace far from the theatre.
But near the corner of Seventh Avenue a round, comfortable little figure of a man, moon-faced and pudgy-
fisted, rolled against him, and he heard, in a moment,
the ingratiating purr of a soft Irish intonation: "Come
to see the little play next week. It's only a bit of craft.
But the 'old man' doesn't let anything fail. It ought

to play to good business. Some day, though, I'm going to write a play I've got in mind and publish it. That'll be my real work. I'll send you . . ."

But the critic had turned swiftly and melted into the more solid darkness farther West.

Marionettes [1]

TOWARD the close of the nineteenth century children and simple folk in Europe still saw the puppets or played with them as unreflectively as their remotest ancestors had done. In windy summers or russet autumns Italians displayed their marionettes in amusement parks far in the North of Europe. The gaudily painted little stage was set up in the open; the benches in front of it were firmly fastened in the earth. The marionettes were rather tall and their movements very angular. But they were all emperors or clowns, very stately or full of the broadest fun, and their robes had once been stiff with brocade and gold. And a child who saw this show with his nurse-maid might then go home and in his play-room snuggle into a curtained box (Punch and Judy Show or Kasperletheater), take the limp dolls, and make very vivid things of them by placing his index finger in the head, his thumb and second finger into the hollow arms, and letting them go through a strange mixture of the old folk-plays and of his own day-dreams.

The child and his nurse-maid did not have to play at make believe. To them there existed no distinction

[1] *The Book of Marionettes.* By Helen Haiman Joseph.

between appearance and reality, feigning and fact.
Their world had not yet been divided between day and
dream. It was of one stuff throughout; they were free
of all its regions and could pass from one to another
without jar. Only by recalling or recovering that state
of mind can we understand the origin and persistence
of the puppets. They belong to the old, old dream
world of myth and ritual and fairy lore. To those who
first fashioned them they were not dolls but men and
gods, like the winged bulls and sphinxes that were first
carved with hands and then adored. To abandon the
modern theatre to them, as mystical enthusiasts would
have us do, would be to give up in this art the slow
gains of the critical intelligence—our one weapon
against delusion and cruelty and dread. But as the
clearest-minded will stop amid the bitter business of the
world to read a fairy tale, so there are moods when the
puppets may take us back to our own childhood and
to the childhood of the race.

The history and aspect of the puppets are both
charmingly recorded by Mrs. Joseph in her *Book of
Marionettes*.[1] She writes with a fantastic, airy touch
that suits her subject, and her illustrations are chosen
with admirable erudition and taste. Puppets have been
found in Thebes and in Attica, but time has dealt
roughly with them. They came from the Orient in the
beginning, and of the true folk marionettes those from

[1] *The Book of Marionettes.* By Helen Haiman Joseph.

the far East are still the best. The rounded marionettes of Java hold the dim dreams and terrors of their
makers, and the wooden puppets of Burma have an
eerie gaiety. The Cingalese puppets are, evidently, of
an incomparable delicacy and precision of workman-
ship. They have a sad and wondering gravity of expression; they were made by a folk that knew strangeness to have a beauty of its own. The shadow figures
of the Eastern islands are grotesque and wildly fierce,
those of China calmer and stealthier in their cruelty;
the puppet-heads of Japan are bland, but behind their
wan smiles lurk fear and horror. All these puppets
were made in faith, in rapt and dreamy earnestness,
and the shows aroused pity and terror.

The Christian centuries put the marionettes to more
definitely religious uses. But side by side with these
the puppets served to embody other figures of the folk
imagination—Pulcinella and Arlecchino, Punch and
Judy, Kasperle and Frau Ritter Pantoflius—which all
betrayed the humor and the realistic spirit of the West.
They persisted through later centuries and presented
popular legends, some recent, some of incredible an-
tiquity, and the booths of the puppet shows were as
regular as jugglers and magicians at festivals and fairs.
It was at such a booth that Goethe in his childhood
saw the puppet play of Doctor Faust, which has been
preserved in the version used at Ulm and illustrates
in its three parts, sub-divided into tiny acts, the char-

acter of the later plays of the puppet shows. But here we are on or very near the dividing line between a more ancient and more modern mood. The latter was soon to drive the puppets out. They do not thrive amid reasoning and motivated actions. They and their spectators must stay within the land of dreams.

Now, of course, no adult can go quite naïvely to a puppet show. It remains a curiosity and an experiment in æsthetic experience. Thus it is significant that the best of the very few theatres devoted to puppets in the world, the Marionetten Theatre Münchner Künstler, is an exponent in miniature of the subtlest and most exquisite devices of the modern craftsmanship of the stage. The marionettes of Mrs. Maurice Browne in the Little Theater in Chicago, those of the Cleveland Playhouse, and of Mr. Tony Sarg in New York all share that sophistication, even when they strive most to approach the simplicity of the old figures. Their makers do not really believe in them and their audiences bring them no creative faith. Only the marionettes of Richard Teschner of Vienna escape this difficulty. He was influenced by the Javanese shadow play. But his little figures have the faintly poignant morbidness of all the costly maladies of the modern soul, and one can imagine them dancing to faint verses of Verlaine or playing the obscurer visions of Hofmannsthal or the moralities of Arthur Symons. But their frail forms would wither in the booths of the market-place.

It is a great pity that the puppets cannot serve some of their ancient uses among the many simple people who are necessarily beyond the reach of the modern art of the theatre. In every village of the land there is a moving-picture show, and the stories told on the screen by the images of real people in real places are of a conscious and malignantly corrupting falseness. In them murder is represented as a small affair, war as a sort of super-football, getting the better of one's neighbor as the chief end of man. The lithe, brown men who still watch the grave faces of their puppet kings and queens act their old legends in Ceylon are far less ignobly deluded. But a realism of means, of reproduction, is confused among us with reality of content, and one wonders whether the villagers of southern Ohio or of the North Carolina mountains would not laugh incredulously at a puppet show that brought them a truth of poetry and of dreams and legends. Perhaps their children would yield themselves to the lure of fairy-plays and thus undergo a cleansing of the imagination. The hope is forlorn as are the puppets themselves in the modern world. But their history is full of fascination and of the infinitely quaint grace expressed by Gounod in his *Funeral March of a Marionette.* With grave, precise, and slightly mincing steps the little figures pass and are lost in the dusk.

Toward a People's Theatre

THE rigid mind resists art. Not, to be sure, all the arts. In music, where medium and substance are identical, each temperament may catch the echo of its own mood. One man, listening to the andante of Beethoven's twenty-third sonata (Op. 37), will hear the austere resignation of a great and lonely mind, another will interpret that majesty and sweetness in a different fashion and see the sky break and show the silver of angelic plumage. But literature is built upon ideas and the drama projects ideas in terms of concrete living. Thus the same people will patronize good music and flock to foolish plays. They are capable of hearing the Symphonia Eroica in the afternoon and going in the evening to see the latest melodrama by Channing Pollock or Elmer Rice in which a foreign villain assails the virtue of American women and is foiled by some pure and heroic district attorney. Or, under the influence of a quite transitory Idol of the Tribe, they are willing to be edified by a third-rate Belgian actor's violent mouthing of the remote, white loveliness of Albert Samain's verses. But if Allan Monkhouse's *Mary Broome* were to be brought from Grand Street to Broadway their resistance to it would be complete and final.

This rigidness of mind is neither voluntary nor conscious. It is an instinctive weapon of defense that belongs to definite groups in the social and economic order. The healthy and comfortable husband, unless he is a born thinker, resents a criticism of marriage; the prosperous business man, criticism of the methods of trade; the self-satisfied father, criticism of parental authority and wisdom. The possessor resists change. To him truth is indeed pragmatic. How can you expect him to endure a vital questioning of all the truths that he has found to pay so well? If he pretends to culture he is willing to be mildly imaginative, and hence the feebler kind of neo-romantic play occasionally interrupts the spiritual sordidness of our theatre. He will lionize the author of *The Bluebird* or of *The Faithful*. The author of *Man and Superman* or of *The Sunken Bell* would fare but ill. He faintly respects the classic writers because the possessive orders against which they rebelled have long been swept away. He would be shocked and suspicious if you told him that, in a period of reaction, John Milton was once pursued for sedition and for having conspired against the government like any ragged communist in yesterday's raid by the Department of Justice. But he is really neither vicious nor stupid. His possessions possess him, and, like Wagner's dragon, he desires to sleep.

These are platitudes. But they are eternal and eternally forgotten. Their acceptance is confused by iso-

lated exceptions of various kinds—the mental flexibility of a small crowd of Londoners in Shakespeare's
time, the revolt of an occasional aristocrat like Shelley.
But such exceptions do not touch the central fact.
Art arises from hunger—hunger for beauty or harmony
or truth or justice. Even when art heals a dissonance,
that dissonance must first have been perceived. How,
then, can it speak to those who are convinced that they
hold beauty and truth and justice in the hollow of their
hand? And to-day, as never before, and in the drama
as in no other art, the great hunger which is also the
great rebellion and the great striving to remold the
world a little nearer to the heart's desire, vibrates in
every voice. Hence our theatre must seek another
audience than that of the possessors merely. It is not
necessary to have any romantic or sentimental illusions about the people; it is quite necessary to remember that among the possessing classes there are many
minds that are deeply troubled and divided. But to
watch the audiences in our fashionable theatres in the
mass is to know that here all hope must be left behind.
These people insist on being confirmed in all they have
and are. It is a popular error that they are tired.
They are magnificently fit and fresh. They have dined
and need no food; they possess all the truth they need
and want no art. What is left? A thrilling yarn of
offenders against their order who are crushed, or clowns,
or dancing girls. Therefore the theatre must go to

those whose world is not complete and perfect, who feel some lack of beauty or justice, whose hunger is akin to the hunger of the creative artist himself, who do not go to the table of art in an equal repletion of body and of soul.

This people's theatre will not and must not be a huge place. It should consist of many small stages in different streets and cities. Its accessories can be simple, since the majority of its productions will require only ordinary modern interiors. It should not charge more than one dollar and a half for any seat and it need not, in small houses, charge less than a dollar for any. It must begin with professional actors, but one of its chief aims should be to find and train gifted persons who shall be willing to practise their beautiful art on modest but regular salaries and hold this worthier than the alternate affluence and squalor of the average actor of the commercial stage. It must have, above all, excellent producing managers. Several little theatres among us that might have become starting-points of a movement toward a folk theatre fail through the eccentricity and incompetence of their producing management. The stages of the People's Theatre will have no room and no time for Cubist decorations or the plays of young persons who have just escaped from a campus and mistake singularity for freedom and distinction.

The productions at the Neighborhood Playhouse are noteworthy examples of what a People's Theatre can

do even under untoward conditions. The players are
unhappily all amateurs. Yet when it is considered
that these young people work for their livelihood during the week, rehearse at night, and play on Saturday
and Sunday, the result is astonishing. They have the
sense of the theatre and they have the sense of life.
Several of them put themselves into their parts with
extraordinary sensitiveness and flexibility. And they
do so, one suspects, because to them, far more than to
the professional actor of Broadway, the form and content of the art of the drama is an immediate and a
native experience of the mind and heart.

The Strolling Players

THE strolling players of Scarron have joined those others who traveled in the car of Thespis. The wandering comedian belongs to a dying race. Yet it dies hard. The instinct of the mime is strong and the roads of the earth are many. We thought we had seen our last company of such players suddenly and somewhat forlornly descend upon a Knights of Pythias hall in a Southern village many years ago, when, behold, in 1914, in Marion, Ohio—as yet unknown to fame—we came upon another boldly strutting through a curious two-act play about a Kentucky colonel, a Yankee villain, and a wronged wife. And two years later, in an amusement park on the straggling outskirts of a larger city of the Middle West, there turned up a strange, brave little troupe playing, of all things, Ibsen's *Ghosts,* and playing it far from contemptibly, before a handful of astonished yokels, a group of tight-lipped priests who had wandered in from a neighboring vicarage, and a large bat that whirred through the barn-like hall and thudded/softly against the hanging lamps. The players slipped away—lonely symbols of an ancient and perishing mode of life and art. There may be still other troupes, shadowy and obscure survivals. No one sets down the story of their doings or their fate. How many people know that, till but the other day, the old show-boats still plied up and down the Ohio River? The crew consisted of actors; the captain was manager and leading man. The boats contained a hall and a stage, dropped anchor at remote landings and lit their lights, and the villagers came on board to see old melodramas acted and to listen to sad stories of the deaths of kings. The late David Graham Phillips introduced a show-boat into his story of Susan Lenox. But his account is tawdry and episodic and no reliable history of these strange craft exists; they have still no Scarron.

It is not the moving picture show that has given the strolling players their coup de grace; it is the road company. The members of these companies are anything but adventurous mimes seeking the open roads of a gay world. They are employees. They might as well be in shops. To them one-night stands in the Canadian Northwest are as stripped of essential adventure as working on the "subway circuit" in Brooklyn or the Bronx. Pullman coaches connect the houses controlled by the theatrical trusts from Alaska to the Gulf of Mexico and the players carry the echoes of last year's Broadway hits from Fargo to Mobile. The wildest of the ancient arts is organized on a nation-wide business basis and seventy-five dollars a week plus railroad expenses paid from the New York office drains the last drop of adventurousness from the player's bones. Tales of stranded road-companies, of shifts and quaint accidents are out of date. All the hotels serve grape-fruit for breakfast and the same dishes with the same names in bad French for dinner. The development of civilization, in flat contradiction of Spencer's definition, is from variety to sameness, and soon the dusty fellow with a collapsible merry-go-round will be the last representative of the wandering mimes who were proud, shabby, and eloquent upon the roads to Babylon and in the shadow of the great cathedrals.

No wonder that romantic souls have been eager somehow to revive the long tradition of the traveling show. From Greenwich Village came last season the announcement of a Caravan Theater. But no one seems to have summoned it. A similar message comes from England this season and they who send it may have better luck. Mr. Stuart Walker's "Portmanteau Theater" remains, however, the typical experiment of its kind. It, too, has left the roads. But for certain seasons it fared up and down the land. Only, alas, it did not go to the people. No square or town-hall was suddenly lifted into passion, poetry, and wonder because of its coming. It was cannily summoned with expenses guaranteed by Drama League centers and women's clubs. It lacked robustness, breadth, and popularity in the nobler sense. The little plays were tenuous and neo-romantic and far more like millinery than like folk-ballads. Later on Mr. Walker gave some superb productions and wrote one very beautiful play. But he was too aloof and also too artful to revive the tradition of the strolling players. If ever we are to have such again, they must be more like Vachel Lindsay in the days when he chanted his rimes for a supper and a night's lodging. They must flee the hot atmosphere of the scented studio and the "little theatre" and all contamination of experts in the decorative arts. A platform, a passion, a burning thought and youth—these are their only needs. Perhaps some day a group of young collegians—we have seen and known possible ones—instead of drifting to schools of acting or "arty" cliques, will take to the road and act both Shakespeare and Ibsen on the Main Streets of towns and villages and redeem hungry souls from the toils and graces of the stars of the "Realart," the "Metro," and the "Universal."

Interlude

THE critic was quite suddenly charged with a duty. He hates duties imposed from without. It is hard enough to meet the obligations dictated from within. He was to take to the theatre a lady whom he had barely met. He surveyed her coldly. Mouse-colored hair, bluish-gray eyes, a faintly agreeable precision and purity of lines, but no curves. Or, rather, all curves were subdued. Her clothes were neither rustic nor innocent. There was a pallid but ordered decorative scheme. A large ring of turquoise brought out the blue of her eyes. Severity is here, the critic reflected, partly a matter of defense; also of deference to a New England ancestry, a doctorate, and the authorship of several learned pamphlets. He was asked for suggestions and reminded that the lady's stay in New York was brief. He firmly named a given evening, promised a surprise, and was rewarded by a smile that was meant to be wintry and ended by being wistful.

He had his first misgiving when he conducted his friend to their seats in the Winter Garden on the opening night of *The Passing Show of 1921*. She admitted that the auditorium was magnificent but glanced nervously at the little glass ash-receivers attached to the backs of the chairs. An obese gentleman on her left smoked an obese cigar; the lady with the diamond necklace in front lit a cigarette. The critic became for a moment false to his own harsh intentions. "I hope the smoke doesn't bother you." Of course she said that it didn't. Next she glanced wonderingly at the bridge which ran from the stage straight through the audience. "The chorus comes out there," the critic explained. He saw his friend's lips grow into mere lines. Suddenly he remembered that one of her pamphlets dealt with the classification of images in Latin poetry. He took a plunge and quoted:

> Gratia cum Nymphis geminisque sororibus audet
> Ducere nuda choros.

She laughed and there was a richer alto tone in the depth of that laughter than he had expected.

She hadn't seen the recent Broadway successes and the parodies bewildered her a little. The critic also knew that her spiritual antennæ quivered perceptibly at the bare knees of the chorus. Nevertheless she admitted—discreet conversation was easy here—that there was something exhilarating in the play of light and color and rhythm. "The rhythmic movement of the lightly draped human body singly or in groups," the critic reminded her, "is not only the oldest but the mother of all the arts." She looked at him with grave

wonder. "I've made that very statement." "Very
well, here is your academic maxim come to life." Just
then the lights grew dim and the chorus, carrying small,
duskily glowing balloons, tripped across the bridge out
into the audience. The lady watched the girls closely
and almost with a quiver. Then she whispered, "I
suppose the artifice saves it. They're like girls in a
picture. Anyway it's lovely." The critic would have
put it differently. But he was well content.

Only the chief comedian, he saw clearly, repelled
her. A hard disdain came into her eyes—something
aloof and feudal. She was building a wall of glass
about her nerves. The critic crashed through. "Ah,
yes," he said, "Howard has a monstrously Semitic nose
and, apparently, a forehead of brass. But remember
the clown must hit the fancy of the populace. We're
not in the Watteau. garden described by Pater; Howard is no Pierrot lunaire. This is New York. Howard's Yiddish jokes offend you. But you see, the
descendants of the Back Bay families run no theatres—
neither the Guild which you so delicately approve nor
the Winter Garden which you are almost ready to endure. This rude farceur and Max Reinhardt of whom
the cultured patter and the divine Sarah whom they
glory to have seen all belong to the same tribe. Howard is, at least, effective. As a trombone, you think?
The Harlequin doesn't play the horns of Elfland." She
turned to the critic with a disarming smile. "I suppose

he *is* funny." "Funny and, as he should be, vulgar.
He wants to reach the profanum vulgus."

During the second part of the entertainment the
learned lady did not speak. Her pupils expanded; her
features softened and glowed. All her life she had been
taken only to the more arid among the "better things."
Intently she watched the magic melting of one exquisitely conventionalized background into another and
watched Cleveland Bronner and Ingrid Solfeng dancing
a vizualization of symbolic dreams. Here a new art
was revealed to her, an art she had known only from
the frozen gestures on some crumbling frieze. It was
allied to music, but less intricate and more primitive—
an art of expression divinely perfect yet wholly natural.
Thus would we all dance if we could and dared and
had the beauty and strength of body and were not the
crippled slaves of routine and ugliness. Thus would
we all, intoxicated by our own fleeting but immortal
rhythms, throw off "the heavy and the weary weight of
all this unintelligible world." And now the critic's
guest gave a little thrilled gasp when in the Firefly bal-
let the innumerable chorus surged in wild rhythmic
lines about Mr. Bronner and a hundred limbs streaming through the changeful lights built up an altitude of
pure motion like the fortissimo of a great orchestra.
And she smiled and even swayed gently when, in later
scenes, two less poetic and imaginative dancers created
with their dry but inimitable nimbleness the moods of

ordinary pleasure and liberation that we meet upon our dusty road.

She insisted on walking to her hotel. All her defenses had broken down. A lock of hair tumbled from under her hat and streamed in the wind. She said good-night with a strange swaying forward of her body. The lines had become curves. She chanted under her breath as she went "Gratia cum Nymphis."

Oasis

THE last week had been hard to bear. It had brought *The Man in the Making,* a burly play for hard-headed business men; it had brought *Wait Till We're Married,* which dealt in lightning-like stage conversions and ended on a smile; it had brought Mr. Edward Childs Carpenter's tepid *Pot Luck,* with glimpses of talent carefully curbed for the box-office. One felt, therefore, quite in one's accustomed element when a stout gentleman whose diamond stickpin was as noisy as his voice asked in the vestibule of the Ambassador Theater: "Music by Schubert, eh? Which is it, Jake or Lee? Never knew those fellows went in for composing." Then one went in and the curtain rose and there—despite a hundred things to rasp the fastidious and those who wisely or unwisely hold themselves aloof from the arts that please the people—there was old Vienna, the city of Gluck, of Mozart, of Beethoven, a city that seemed not only to lend a home to genius but to give that genius a touch of divine felicity and serenity; there, somewhat in his manner as he lived, was Franz Schubert.

The operetta named *Blossom Time* and presented in a new Broadway theatre was, of course, the famous

Drei Mädelhaus, which, after a resounding success in
Europe, had reached the Irving Place Theater in the
winter of 1918. Its performance by the German stock
company there was shabby to the eye and not important musically. But a breath of poetry and pathos, of
earnestness and desiderium passed through it which
was sought in vain amid the magnificent mountings and
admirable voices at the Ambassador.

Professional devotees of music—and devotees of
music are apt to be a little professional—would not be
pleased, one saw at once, with the whole scheme of
Blossom Time. They might merely disdain the act of
building a play around the life of Franz Schubert. But
to trick out that play with Schubert's songs, to ring all
possible changes on the everlasting Ständchen, to use
the great melody from the Unfinished Symphony quite
as the leit-motif and enveloping tune is used in the
cheapest music shows! Yes, it was barbarous. And
the American production added new atrocities to the
old. The tempo of the loveliest of the Wiener Walzer
was shamelessly accelerated—"jazzed up" is the better
expression—and, at the end of the second act, the melody from the D-minor was suddenly dovetailed into
that of *Ich schnitt es gern in jede Rinde ein,* which is
probably the feeblest, though one of the most popular
of the four hundred songs. It need only be added that
the Ave Maria was used as a "number" called Lonely
Hearts, and that in the midst of a musical pattern

hopelessly at variance with it we seemed to detect several measures of the exquisite Forelle. There was nothing to set off against these things except the fact that the Military March was played with the nicest regard for Schubert's intention. To which praise our more terrible musical friends at once replied: Yes, but his intention in this instance was quite unmusical and popular and unfortunately happens not to interest us at all.

Very well. But when, on leaving the theatre, we heard the usher call out: "All the hits of the show at forty cents apiece!" and saw the honest bourgeois with still glowing faces crowd forward to buy "the hits of the show," we felt certain that the American producers of the *Drei Mädelhaus* had done a good deed—vital, beautiful, beneficent. It is easy and lends you an air of pleasing originality and saves you from the reproach of priggishness if, having just come from Mengelberg, you say: "Ah, yes, I find rag-time most interesting. It's an original contribution to music. Irving Berlin is a very clever chap." It is easy and rather disgusting. Out in the land beside a hundred thousand pianos and phonographs the young gather in the evening. And among these young people are also students and especially the students of the great State universities. And the pianos tinkle and the phonographs croak "When the midnight shoo-shoo leaves for Alabam'" or "Honey Boy, I hate to see you leavin'" and the hits from the latest Broadway successes by Mr. Otto Harbach or Mr. Silvio Hein and, at most and best, some sugary, rhetorical, fundamentally soulless bit from an Italian opera. But suppose *Blossom Time* achieves the sweeping success which it promised to achieve and in cottages and fraternity houses from coast to coast the pianos and phonographs play the Wiener Walzer! Listen to it with your inner ear in its original tempo as the words glide past the eye:

> Und unter blühendem Flieder
> Mit duftendem Mieder,
> Die Eine, die Feine, die meine muss sein!

What soft gaiety through which breaks the eternal sadness of the soul, what infinite grace, how spiritual a rhythm, what yearning, what delight! Yes, we insist that this time, if not before, the Messrs. Shubert showed themselves public benefactors and wiped out a multitude of their quite unquestionable sins.

And so at the risk of seeming incorrigibly barbarous we express the final hope that *Blossom Time* will be followed by a Beethoven operetta called *Adelaide,* and by one woven of the songs of Robert Schumann. The critics of music may sneer. But if phonograph records of *Mondnacht* and *Frühlingsnacht* and *Der Kranke* and *Der Wanderer* were played in every Main Street "home" and every lonely farmhouse, what should we care for the words of critics? Think of the delight that would be spread and the souls that would be saved.

Underworld

AMERICAN literature is said to be looking up. Discounting the wilder claims and prophecies, one may gladly admit a vigorous stir in poetry and in criticism. If the production of sound fiction, novels that are both creative and true, is still small, one can at least dismiss all anxiety for this branch of literary art. No American novel that has distinction or promise need go begging. The publishers yearn and pray for such manuscripts and will leave their offices in search of them. A different story must be told of the drama. If an American playwright of the caliber of, let us say, Dreiser or Hergesheimer, the Strindberg-Hauptmann or the Donnay-Schnitzler type were to appear, he would not perhaps be mute; he would assuredly be inglorious.

He would, quite naturally, come to New York to see the managers. He would find them heavily guarded by underlings and excessively elusive. He would be told to leave his "script" and given a perfunctory assurance that it would be examined. Then an empty silence would fall upon him. He would seek to break this silence by telephoning or by repeating his call at the

manager's office. In vain. Publishers can be reasoned
with, since they can be seen. Managers melt into thin
air. Our American dramatist, presumably young, would
sink into a kind of limbo of the spirit—a gray and forlorn region. Recalling the glow of creation and the
deep urgency of his ambition, he would seek to find
other roads to the theatre. He would be aware of the
fact that two or three dramatic critics in America spend
their strength doing battle for precisely the kind of play
he has written. To these he will now address himself.
He will ask George Jean Nathan or even the humble
writer of these words to read his manuscript and will
be bitterly disappointed by the result. Yet the critic
is quite helpless. How is he to know that this particular play is a masterpiece? He must either read all
manuscript plays that come to him or none. Since
life itself forbids the former course and since discrim-
ination would be both unjust and futile, he chooses the
latter. He does so the more calmly as he knows his
influence with managers to be almost wholly limited to
suggesting the kind of thing they already want. Mr.
J. D. Williams's production of Eugene O'Neil's *Beyond
the Horizon* offers a solitary exception. But O'Neil's
one-act plays had previously been given a hearing
through the Provincetown Players, and profited by the
circumstance that Mr. Nathan prints one-act plays in
the *Smart Set*. To Mr. Arthur Hopkins and to the
Theatre Guild our stage owes inestimable benefits. The

production of a single seriously good play of native origin was not until recently among them.

Our young dramatist, shivering in his hall bed-room, will now remember as a last resort that playwrights and players have often worked together. He will seek out prominent actors and actresses. If by virtue of social adroitness, a gift for flattery, and an ingratiating manner—qualities likely to be his in inverse ratio to his talent and nobility of purpose—he succeeds in interviewing "stars," he will find, first, that they are commonly "owned" by managers quite as baseball players are and have to play in the plays provided, and, secondly, that they themselves are not looking for good plays, but for grateful and preposterously showy parts. This point they will make clear to him with a gigantic and unblushing simplicity of mind.

In these fruitless efforts our dramatist will have spent at least six months. A dullness will have fallen upon his spirit; his fastidiousness and sensitiveness will show rents and callouses. In his rooming-house, at restaurants, on Broadway itself, in the reception rooms of managers, he hears interminable talk concerning the art and business by which plays are "gotten on." A tall, youngish man is encouraging. He is about to have a play produced by a new manager. It took him eight years. An elderly person with a moist sputter and a crumpled face is bleak on the whole subject. Years ago he was co-author of a successful

farce. Now he broods bitterly over a trunkful of un-
produced plays. Our young dramatist shudders, but
he listens. He has nothing else to do. "You've got
to give the managers what they want." "Yes, but what
do they want?" The feeble talk eddies back and forth.
Somebody says in a rough, tired, oracular voice: "Alf.
Stone's secretary once said to me, says he: 'What the
boss wants is melodramas to make people die of fright
or bedroom farces to make 'em die laughin'.' " Our
dramatist happens to come upon another group. Here
the talk is of the gorgeous profits of the gilded hacks,
of the fabulous fees paid by the great film corporations
for scenarios and "movie rights." "Yes," some one
says, " 'is all right. But there's no use submitting scenarios. They steal 'em. You got to get next." That
phrase throbs in our dramatist's aching head. It sums
up his situation. He has spent his years on the noblest
of the arts, not on the art of "getting next." But concerning his art he has not heard a syllable spoken. He
has slipped into an underworld of spiritual prostitution.
These people watch the plays with the largest box-office
receipts. These they imitate. Then they fawn and
cajole and treat underlings to luncheon and wait weary
hours in managers' offices to "get next." Swiftly our
dramatist walks to the office of the manager who has
had his play for the past five weeks. He demands his
manuscript. A young woman with rosy nails and bril-
liantined hair fetches it languidly from an inner sanc-

tuary. No interest has been shown. No report communicated. He has not "gotten next."

This account is no fanciful one. It is based on hard facts. It may be replied that we have no American dramatists of the nobler kind. But how are we to tell? It is certain that a young Ibsen or Hauptmann or Shaw would meet in New York to-day the fate described and would withdraw in just and austere wrath to his native province. Those that remain and sink into the underworld of the theatre and at last succeed on its terms are not they for whom we are waiting or whom our drama needs.